THE ETERNAL YEAR

THE ETERNAL YEAR

by

KARL RAHNER, S.J.

Translated by John Shea, S.S.

HELICON

BALTIMORE—DUBLIN

Helicon Press, Inc.
1120 N. Calvert Street
Baltimore, Maryland 21202

264.02

Library of Congress Catalog Card Number 64-20233

originally published in German under the title
Kleines Kirchenjahr by Verlag Ars Sacra Josef Müller, Munich, 1953.

Nihil Obstat: Carroll E. Satterfield
               Censor Librorum

Imprimatur: ✠Lawrence J. Shehan, D.D.
               Archbishop of Baltimore
               June 11, 1964

The *Nihil Obstat* and *Imprimatur* are official declarations that a
book or pamphlet is free of doctrinal or moral error. No implica-
tion is contained therein that those who have granted the *Nihil
Obstat* and *Imprimatur* agree with the opinions expressed.

PRINTED IN THE REPUBLIC OF IRELAND BY
CAHILL AND COMPANY LIMITED DUBLIN

CONTENTS

TRANSLATOR'S PREFACE

THE WRITINGS of Karl Rahner testify clearly to his all-consuming and all-pervading singleness of purpose: the quest for reality, the desire to penetrate to the "heart of the matter." His starting point for an investigation might be phrased in the words, "What does it all mean, *really* mean?" Christian reality is the inexhaustible mine of his endeavors, and his goal is to draw out for the men of his age the implications, importance, and significance of Christian reality.

Part of Christian reality is the Church's liturgical year. To this area of the Church's life Karl Rahner, in *The Eternal Year*, directs his energies and his insights. This is not, however, a commentary on the individual texts used by the Church throughout the year. Familiarity with these texts is presupposed; they can never be by-passed, and the more acquainted one is with them, the more striking and personally meaningful will the author's insights be. Nor is this work a collection of meditations only vaguely inspired by the liturgical texts. Rather, the author trains his attention on one or another aspect of the feasts and seasons, from Advent to All Saints, probes into them, and draws out, unfolds and makes clear the significance of each one.

While following the author's development, the reader will do well always to keep in mind the basic unifying event of the Church year, which is Easter. All the feasts, all the seasons, point to and draw their power from Easter, for the celebration of Easter is the celebration par excellence of the event that the Church is always celebrating, the death and resurrection, the paschal mystery, the center, the heart, the core of christianity. For it is the celebration of an event that belongs to the Person of the Word made flesh, to the risen Lord who has triumphed once and for all over sin, death, and Satan. Easter is the center of the Church year because it is the risen, glorified Christ who stands behind the diversity of feasts and seasons, just as he stands behind all the other manifold realities that constitute Christianity. It is the Person of Christ who unites all things in himself, not melting them down and fusing them into a strange alloy, but filling them with his power, with his life, with his own Spirit. The one irreducible reality of christianity, indeed of history, is the Person of Christ, the God-man and all that he did and now does for us and for our salvation. In a certain sense, when you say "Christ" you say "christianity." He it is who unifies all else that has happened, that now happens, and that will happen.

To understand what bearing this has on Father Rahner's reflections on the Church year, it is necessary to consider for a moment the inter-action of the risen Christ and his Church in the liturgy.

Christ lives now, risen in glory, seated at the Father's right hand, and all that he did on earth has been eternalized in him, so that we can say that it lives on in him now. The Incarnation remains in his eternally meaningful humanity. His death and resurrection, the central events of his life, remain always significant, continually operative, irrevocably necessary for the influx of God's life into the men of all ages, and for the drawing of all men into God's own family life.

But in the era of the Church, from Pentecost to Christ's return, Christ also lives on in the Church. The Church is the great sacrament of Christ, making him present in and to the world. Christ and the Church act together upon men, so that Christ, the eternal God-man, may do for men of all ages what he has already done for his own human nature, that is, give them life—risen, eternal life, the life of God himself. Especially when she celebrates the sacraments, does Christ act together with his Church, reaching out in baptism, for example, to touch a man, and make of him a new creature, bringing him from death to new life, from Satan's dominion into the Church, the kingdom of Christ. Or again, in penance, it is Christ who heals his fallen member, restoring him to the life of the Church, to his own life, which we call grace. It is Christ who baptizes, Christ who absolves; it is Christ who is present and working among men in the Church.

In the Eucharist the Church possesses the total, living Christ of the present, the risen Lord with his eternal sacrifice, his eternal priesthood, his eternal victimhood. The risen life that he now lives, obtained through his death, he pours out upon us most fully through the Eucharist, the sun and center of the sacramental world. Here is the source of all life, here is the sacrament that unifies all else. But we are still limited by the time and space of earthly flesh. We cannot think of or experience everything at once; so we cannot appreciate the Eucharist all at once. *For our sakes* the one single vivifying reality, compressed and concentrated in the Eucharist, is broken down through the Church's liturgical year. God does not need feasts and seasons; we do.

It is as if one strong dazzling beam of light shone down upon us from the risen Lord; this beam is refracted and diffused for our weak eyes through the spectrum of the Church year. Just as we cannot see the richness of the colors contained in a single beam of sunlight unless it is sent through a prism, so too the Church year shows us all the different aspects, all the richness and glory of the one, central, all-embracing, unifying event of the Lord's death and resurrection, which we call the paschal mystery, which we celebrate in the Eucharist.

For this reason the Church has her different seasons, her variety of feasts; for this reason she celebrates the death and resurrection of the Lord in so many different ways: at Easter and in Holy Week, in the Ascension and at Pentecost, at Christmas and Epiphany, in Advent and Lent, in other feasts of the Lord, in those of his mother, and of his saints. The Church year is a precious diamond in the hands of our mother the Church; slowly she turns it around, so that we may see every facet, every aspect of it. It is one stone—Easter—with many facets: all the feasts.

Finally, the reader should recall that paradox is part and parcel of the Church's nature as she makes her way over all the dusty roads of this earth towards her goal, the last day. Like her master before his "hour" of exaltation through death and resurrection, she is eternal, yet dwells in time; she is spirit, yet she lives in flesh; she is already the heavenly city, yet she sojourns now on earth, tied down and hemmed in by space; she is above history, yet she is immersed in it. Time and eternity, space and infinity, spirit and flesh—these are always with the Church as she journeys through history towards her "hour," when the Lord shall come again. In the era of the Church these tensions are not yet completely resolved, they are not eliminated; but they are radically resolved through her faith in the risen Christ, for he has gone before her, and she sees in him what she will one day be. It is faith that enables her to perceive heavenly realities while she still dwells on earth. But faith is more than seeing, more than conceptual knowledge. In the Church, and so in each member, faith is the living bond between heaven and earth, between time and eternity, the bond that makes us be already what we must become through life: citizens of the heavenly city, living stones of the new and eternal city of the living God.

The eternal in time, the infinite in space, the Word made flesh, unity in diversity, Christian faith—these are the main lines of the tapestry which Karl Rahner weaves from the rich, colorful threads of his insights into the eternal year of the Church.

John M. Shea, S.S.

I

ADVENT

We begin today the season of Advent. The term "Advent" connotes not only an arrival, but also that which is yet to come. The very word itself expresses a strange interpenetration of the present and the future, of what now exists and what is yet to come, of possession and expectation. So too, in the liturgy of Advent, the present and the future of christian salvation are mysteriously interwoven. The incarnation of the Word of God took place in the past and still continues in the present. Christ's return to judge all men and to complete his redeeming work is an event of the future, and yet he is constantly on the point of coming. The expectation of this return and the memorial of his entrance into the world are both celebrated in the liturgy.

At one and the same time the Advent liturgy's remembrance unites all of these within itself. It unites the past, i.e., the Old Testament longing for the coming of the salvation that was still hidden in God alone; the present, i.e., the salvation that is now taking place in the world but which is still hidden in Christ; and the future, i.e., the salvation that will be unveiled with the transformation of the world at the end of time. The Church must make memorial of and re-experience all three mysterious stages of salvation history. The inwardness of the salvation-less past must remain, because otherwise we would not be aware of what we are when we are left to ourselves alone, and because we would otherwise forget that if we are to possess God's grace, it must come to us from him alone. The inwardness of the salvation that is already taking place and being accomplished must remain, because it is ours only if we have grasped it in faith as that which belongs to us in the present. The inwardness of the future must remain, because the present is present only if we have seized it as the earnest that promises definitive redemption.

Through the work of God in Christ, time has become what it was supposed to be. Time is no longer the bleak, empty, fading succession of moments, one moment destroying the preceding one and causing it to become "past," only to die away itself, clearing the way for the future that presses— itself already mortally wounded. Time itself is redeemed. It possesses a center that can preserve the present and gather into itself the future, a nucleus that fills the present with a future that is already really effected, a focal point that co-ordinates the living present with the eternal future. The advent of the incarnate God, of the Christ who is the same yesterday and today and in eternity (Heb 13:8), from whom neither the things of the present nor of the future can separate those who believe in him and who are united with him in love (Rom 8:38, 39)—this advent has penetrated into this time that is to be redeemed.

From this vantage point we shall once again, during this Advent, grasp more deeply what advent-faith is, and thus make our hearts ready for it. Our conception of the christian faith is often too one-sided. We conceive it only as a set list of determined facts that must be held as true. These facts stand by themselves on this list, and we just think about them. These facts, however, are fundamentally an event that still endures. We are situated right in the midst of this event, and we are, precisely through faith, drawn into it, so that we are caught up in it.

to here Turn to p. 17

In the present time of faith, we do not merely take notice of an event, an eternal reality, that happened only once, some time ago. We do not only notice that "later" (in a future that now is entirely unreal) something shall once again happen in salvation history. The believer does not only have certain thoughts and opinions about something, thoughts which remain separate from the event thought about. His "outlook on life" does not merely look upon something that remains external to him and that should be represented in him only by his thoughts about it. In faith the believer "thinks" not only his "thoughts." Faith is more than this: in and through us and our freedom, faith is God's grace working to assimilate the very reality of the event thought about.

By means of faith the salvation of the believer really takes place in the believer himself. Salvation itself comes out from the past into his present, into him, and it becomes present in his time. Christ lives in him. The believer becomes subject to the inner law of each event that is believed. In a mysterious way he becomes a contemporary of the incarnate Son of God. He dies and lives with him. The reason is that through faith Christ lives, in the Holy Spirit, in the believer. Furthermore, in all truth and all reality, this Spirit is gradually shaping the life of the believer into the image of the life and destiny of the incarnate Word of the Father.

Moreover, by this very fact, Christ is in a mysterious way already present in the believer as his future. This future has already come into the believer in a hidden way; he is already, in a hidden way, what he will be when all that is now hidden is unveiled. What will one day be our complete perfection has already begun. And this reality begins precisely because we believe. It is by faith that we are the people of God and children of eternal life, in whom the strength of eternity has already become an operative reality. This one event that is "now" taking place in the world began with the incarnation of God's Son (which was the real, not merely conceptual, reconciliation of God and the world). This event will be completed with Christ's "Second Coming," which is not so much a second arrival as a bringing to perfect completion God's own life already established in the world by the Christ event. This event permeates the believer to the extent that he believes and loves. The believer already possesses his future because his future *is* Christ, and Christ is in the believer. The believer hopes for and awaits his future not as something yet to come which is still unreal, but rather, because he believes, as an event that is happening right now and is developing into his own perfect completion that is to be unveiled.

During this Advent season, let us be more earnest men of faith. Such a season, coming between autumn and winter, can invite us to a livelier awareness of faith, if there is at least a grain of faith already in us. As the autumn season fades and winter begins, the world becomes still. Everything around us turns pale and drab. It chills us. We are least inclined towards gay, hectic activities. More than in other seasons of the year, we prefer to stay home and be alone. It is as if the world had become subdued and had lost the courage to assert its self-satisfaction, the courage to be proud of its power and of its life. Its progressive growth in the swelling fullness of the spring and summer has failed, for the fullness has again vanished. And the fact that the next spring will once again bring a new growth only more strikingly draws our attention to the endless coming and going of the seasons, in which nothing seems to be really permanent, if indeed the approaching winter has as much real significance for us as spring and summer. In this season, time itself bears eloquent witness to its own poverty. It disappoints us. It cannot maintain itself. What it seems to extract from the future and draw into its present is constantly slipping away from it into the past.

Here is the moment to conquer the melancholy of time, here is the moment to say softly and sincerely what we know by faith. This is the season for the word of faith to be spoken in faith: "I believe in the eternity of God who has entered into our time, my time. Beneath the wearisome coming and going of time, life that no longer knows death is already secretly growing. It is already there, it is already in me, precisely because I believe. For the cycle of birth and death to stand still in the true reality all I have to do is believe in the coming of God into our time, really believe. In the act of believing, I patiently bear with time, with its hard and bitter demand that brings death in its wake. And I dwell no longer on the thought that time has the last word to say, which is a denial.

"Listen, my heart, God has already begun to celebrate in the world and in you his Advent. He has taken the world and its time to his heart, softly and gently, so softly that we can miss it. He has even planted his own incomprehensible life in this time (we call it his eternity and we mean thereby that which is nameless, which is wholly other from the time that makes us so hopelessly sad). And this is precisely what happens in you yourself, my heart. It is called the grace of faith, the grace of the gradual falling away of fear of time, of the fear that fades away because he who is more powerful than time (which he made to be redeemed into eternity) has done great things to it. A now of eternity is in you, a now that no longer has any denial before it or behind it. And this now has already begun to gather together your earthly moments into itself.

"No brighter joy could be expected by you, poor heart, in a season of Advent that lasts for a lifetime (since *your* advent will end only when you hear the words, 'enter into the joy of your Lord'). No brighter joy, for now you still feel too keenly the harsh press of the shackles of time, even though they have already begun to fall away from your hands and feet. The only thing that must live in you is a humble, calm joy of faithful expectancy which does not imagine that the tangibles of the present time are everything. Only humble joy, like the joy of a prisoner, who will stand up even while he is still imprisoned, because, lo and behold, the bolt has already been torn off the door of his dungeon, and so freedom is already guaranteed.

"Is this joy, this advent joy so difficult? Is resignation and hidden despair really easier? Childish, stubborn defiance and willed malice: that is what despair and resignation amount to. You rightly recognize these, my heart, only when you run away from them, only when you do not dawdle and dispute with them. Only the heart that really does not want to enjoy them, but instinctively recoils and runs from them under the impulse of that eternal life that we call grace—only such a heart can recognize them. But perhaps you don't quite know whether you have chosen Advent joy or the despair of winter that leads to cold death? Just to ask such a question is a mistake, because we can never be neutral about this when we ask it. And to give the second answer would be death, the death that man cannot free himself from.

"Ask not, doubt not. You have, my heart, already chosen the joy of Advent. As a force against your own uncertainty, bravely tell yourself, 'It is the Advent of the great God.' Say this with faith and love, and then both the past of your life, which has become holy, and your life's eternal, boundless future will draw together in the now of this world. For then into the heart comes the One who is himself Advent, the Boundless Future who is already in the process of coming, the Lord himself, who has already come into the time of the flesh to redeem it."

II

CHRISTMAS

THE CELEBRATION of Christmas is such a pious custom! The
Christmas tree, the pretty presents, the excitement of the
children and a little Christmas music are always beautiful
and touching. A religious mood intensifying the atmosphere
makes it especially lovely and touching. To be sure, we are
all secretly a little self-indulgent—who will blame us?—and
so we readily let ourselves fall into a mood that is peaceful
and comforting, just as we pat a crying child on the head and
say, "It isn't so bad, everything will surely turn out all
right."

Is this all there is to Christmas? Is this the main point?
Or are the beauty and coziness, the stillness and intimacy of
Christmas only the fine, gentle echo of an event that is
today's real celebration, an event that takes place somewhere
else altogether, much higher in heaven, much deeper in the
abysses, and much more inwardly in the soul? Are the joy
and peace of Christmas only the expression of a mood, in
which one dreamily takes refuge? Or are they the outward
expression marking the sacred celebration of an actual event?
Even if we should not want it to be true, even if we grasp no
more from it than a little childlike romanticism and homey
comfort, Christmas is by all means truth and reality. In the
face of it we bravely open our hearts so that it may also
happen to us and through us.

Christmas is more than a bit of cheerful mood. The child—

he is the one who counts today. The important figure in this holy night is the child, the one child, the Son of God, and his birth. Everything else about this feast is based on and quickened by this, or else it dies and turns to illusion. Christmas means that he has come. He has made the night bright. He has turned the night of our darkness, our incomprehensible night, into Christmas. The terrible night of our anxiety and helplessness is now a holy night. This is what Christmas tells us. Through this feast, the moment when this event took place once and for all should also become a reality in our hearts and should remain there to form our entire outlook on life, our *christian* outlook.

If we mortals are completely immersed in the average experiences of our blind, routine, monotonous daily life, then we will have to come to the frightening and discouraging view that—in small things and great—nothing of importance really happens in the world. To be sure, we might think that there is an eternal rise and fall of world-events, of the destiny of nations, even of personal experiences, sometimes good and joyful, usually bad and gloomy. Ultimately, however, all this circles in upon itself, aimlessly and without direction. It wastes away blindly and without meaning. People hide the senseless purposelessness of events only by anxiously taking care not to think beyond the next day. Seen only from our point of view, we are an enigma, an eternally frightening and mortal enigma.

If we should examine the birth of the child of today's feast merely from our point of view, then we could say of him and of us, too, only what is written in the dismal, bitter text of Job 14: "Man, born of woman, is short-lived, heavy with cares; he blossoms like the flower, wilts, is gone like a shadow, and does not last." From our point of view, we could be no more than a tiny point of light in the unlimited dark, a point of light that can only make the darkness even more frightening. We would be no more than a sum that didn't come out right. We seem cast off into time, which makes everything disappear, forced into existence without being asked, laden with wearisome toil and disappointment. Through our own fault we burden ourselves with pain and punishment. We begin to suffer death in the moment when we are born. We are insecure and driven to be childish about all that is illusory, all that is called the sunny side of life—which in reality should be only the refining means of ensuring that the martyrdom and torture of life do not end too quickly.

But if in faith we say, "It is Christmas"—in faith that is determined, sober, and above all else courageous—then we mean that an event came bursting into the world and into our life, an event that has changed all that we call the world and our life. This event alone has provided a goal and a purpose for everything. It has not only put an end to the saying of Ecclesiasticus that there is nothing new under the sun, but also to the Eternal Return of modern philosophers; it is an event through which our night—the fearful, cold, bleak night where body and soul await death from exposure—has become Christmas, the holy night. For the Lord is there, the Lord of creatures and of my life. He no longer merely looks down from the endless "all in one and once for all" of his eternity upon my constantly changing life that glides by far below him. The eternal has become time, the Son has become man, the eternal Purpose of the world, the all-embracing Meaningfulness of all reality has become flesh.

Through this fact, that God has become man, time and human life are changed. Not to the extent that he has ceased to be himself, the eternal Word of God himself, with all his splendor and unimaginable bliss. But he has really become man. And now this world and its very destiny concern him. Now it is not only his work, but a part of his very self. Now he no longer watches its course as a spectator; he himself is now within it. What is expected of us is now expected of him; our lot now falls upon him, our earthly joy as well as the wretchedness that is proper to us. Now we no longer need to seek him in the endlessness of heaven, where our spirit and our heart get lost. Now he himself is on our very earth, where he is no better off than we and where he receives no special privileges, but our every fate: hunger, weariness, enmity, mortal terror and a wretched death. That the infinity of God should take upon itself human narrowness, that bliss should accept the mortal sorrow of the earth, that life should take on death—this is the most unlikely truth. But only this —the obscure light of faith—makes our nights bright, only this makes them holy.

God has come. He is there in the world. And therefore everything is different from what we imagine it to be. Time is transformed from its eternal onward flow into an event that with silent, clear resoluteness leads to a definitely determined goal wherein we and the world shall stand before the unveiled face of God. When we say, "It is Christmas," we mean that God has spoken into the world his last, his deepest, his most beautiful word in the incarnate Word, a word that can no longer be revoked because it is God's definitive deed, because it is God himself in the world. And this word means: I love you, you, the world and man. This is a wholly unexpected word, a quite unlikely word. For how can this word be spoken when both man and the world are recognized as dreadful, empty abysses? But God knows them better than we. And yet he has spoken this word by being himself born as a creature. The very existence of this incarnate Word of love demands that it shall provide, eye to eye and heart to heart, an almost unbelievable fellowship, an *admirabile commercium*, between the eternal God and us. Indeed, it says that this commercium is already there. This is the word that God has spoken in the birth of his Son.

And now there is stillness in the world only for a little while. The busyness that is proudly called universal history, or one's own life, is only the stratagem of an eternal love that wills to enable man to give a free answer to its final word. And in this prolonged short moment of God's silence that is called history after the birth of Christ, man is supposed to have a chance to speak. In the trembling of his heart that quivers because of God's love, he should tell God, who as man stands beside him in silent expectation, "I"—no, rather he should say nothing to him, but silently give himself to the love of God that is there because the Son is born.

Christmas means that God has come to us, come to us in such a way that from now on, even in his own awesome, glorious splendor, he can only be "at home" with the world and with us. Through the birth of this child everything is already transformed. With the inexorability of love, every-thing is already pushing out from that inmost center of reality which is the incarnate Word. It is pushing out towards the countenance of God, and now we need not fear that before God's countenance the world will have to be burned to nothing by his consuming fire of holiness and righteousness. All time is already embraced by the eternity that has itself become time. All tears are dried up at their source, because God himself has wept with them, and has already wiped them from his eyes. All hope is already real possession, because God is already possessed by the world. The night of the world has become bright. God does not allow our stubborn defiance and weakness to be greater than our hearts, and so will not have it be as small as a tiny child who is born and who lies in a crib. Our heart does not want to admit that midnight is already past and that a day without evening already penetrates the night. All bitterness is only the reminder that it is not yet clearly known that the one world-Christmas has dawned; and all the happiness of this earth is only the mysterious confirmation, which most people do not understand, that Christmas is already present.

The feast of Christmas is therefore not poetry and childish romanticism, but the avowal and the faith, which alone justifies man, that God has risen up and has already spoken his final word in the drama of history, no matter how much clamor the world keeps up. The celebration of Christmas can only be the echo of that word in the depth of our being by which we speak a believing "Amen" to God's word that has come from his vast eternity into the narrowness of this world, and yet has not ceased to be the word of God's truth and the word of his own blissful love. When not only the glimmer of candles, the joy of children and the fragrance of the Christmas tree but the heart itself answers God's childlike word of love with a gracious "yes," then Christmas really takes place, not only in mood, but in the most unalloyed reality. For this word of the heart is then truly produced by God's holy grace; God's word is then born in our heart, too. God himself then moves into our heart, just as he moved into the world in Bethlehem, just as truly and really, and yet even more intimately. When the heart itself answers, we really open its gates high and wide, and God comes and takes possession of our hearts, just as in the first Christmas he came and took possession of the world.

And now he says to us what he has already said to the world as a whole through his grace-filled birth: "I am there. I am with you. I am your life. I am your time. I am the gloom of your daily routine. Why will you not bear it? I weep your tears—pour yours out to me, my child. I am your joy. Do not be afraid to be happy, for ever since I wept, joy is the standard of living that is really more suitable than the anxiety and grief of those who think they have no hope. I am the blind alleys of all your paths, for when you no longer know how to go any further, then you have reached me, foolish child, though you are not aware of it. I am in your anxiety, for I have shared it by suffering it. And in doing so, I wasn't even heroic according to the wisdom of the world. I am in the prison of your finiteness, for my love has made me your prisoner. When the totals of your plans and of your life's experiences do not balance out evenly, I am the unsolved remainder. And I know that this remainder, which makes you so frantic, is in reality my love, that you do not yet understand. I am present in your needs. I have suffered them and they are now transformed, but not obliterated from my heart. I am in your lowest fall, for today I began to descend into hell. I am in your death, for today I began to die with you, because I was born, and I have not let myself be spared any real part of this death.

"Do not be sorry, as Job was, for those who are born; for all who accept my salvation are born in this holy night because my Christmas embraces all your days and all your nights. I myself—my whole being and my whole personality —are truly engaged in the terrifying adventure that begins with your birth. I tell you, mine was no easier and no less dangerous than yours. I assure you, though, it had a happy ending. Ever since I became your brother, you are as near to me as I am to myself. If, therefore, I, as a creature, want to prove in me and in you, my brothers and sisters, that I, as Creator, have not made a hopeless experiment with the human race, who then shall tear my hand away from you? I accepted you when I took my human life to myself. As one of your kind, as a fresh start, I conquered in my failure.

"If you judge the future only according to yourselves, you cannot be pessimistic enough. But do not forget that your real future is my present, the present that began today and shall never again become transitoriness. And so you are certainly planning in a realistic way if you rely on my optimism, which is not Utopia but the reality of God. This reality—incomprehensible wonder of my all-mighty love—I have sheltered, safely and completely, in the cold stable of your world. I am there. I no longer go away from this world, even if you do not see me now. When you, poor mortals, celebrate Christmas, then say to everything that is there and to everything that you are, one thing only—say to me: 'You are here. You have come. You have come into everything. Even into my soul. Even behind the stubbornness of my wickedness, which doesn't want to let itself be pardoned.' Say only one thing, and then it is Christmas for you, too; say only: 'You are here.' No, don't say anything. I am there. And ever since then my love is unconquerable. I am there. It is Christmas. Light the candles. They have more right to exist than all the darkness. It is Christmas, Christmas that lasts forever."

III

NEW YEAR'S DAY

TODAY, DEAR christians, we celebrate New Year's Day. Even though the liturgy celebrates the circumcision of the Lord, let us not hesitate to use the secular marking of a new year to stimulate us to solidly christian thoughts. After all, whatever is human is also christian. Since we, too, are human, this is New Year's Day for us, too. As far as we are concerned, the year begins on January first rather than on the first Sunday of Advent. (Historians of the liturgy are not yet sure whether the Church year begins with Advent or not.)

In the business world, the first few days of the new year are given over to the closing and balancing of the books. If in an agraphon the Lord says that we are supposed to be good money changers, then on New Year's we may be permitted to try to take something like a "balance" of our whole life. We can attempt it, for in our time—on New Year's eve—we old people are quite alone; that night the young people are somewhere else. We can, then, calmly look back over the many years that we have already lived; the present day warns us of their fleetingness, and of their significance.

In festive seasons such as this one, we are inclined to let past and present become glazed over by a cheerful glitter of holiday ideals. But this is dangerous, because it easily turns into a sham. When we once pass the peak of life, nobody asks us about our ideals; but rather they ask about our accomplishments: not about what we would like to do, but about what we do. And, at our age, we are no longer readily given the chance still to become what we are not yet.

So there is really nothing left for us to do except to draw up a kind of "balance" of our life, sensibly and seriously. We do this with the expectation that during the coming year many addresses may be crossed off the mailing list. We do this with the uneasy feeling—is it hope or fear?—that everything can still change, because we certainly have not carefully looked into and around all the nooks of our journey through life. Moreover, in spite of the experience we have had of ourselves, we still do not really know who we now actually are. Dear Lord! what surprises can life still hold, what surprises can we still try to get ready for? We draw up this balance with the probability (which almost borders on certainty) that in death we shall be what we now already are, with the certainty, then, that we are old. Yes, my friends, this magnificent insight, that we are old, shall be all that I as the "examiner of the books" shall be able to add to our "balance." But it seems to me that this fact is important, and obscure enough, to permit me a few minutes of your time.

We are already rather old. Now, certainly, it is hardly deniable that this is so in the externals, in business and professional life. Death is always close to man, but not every man lives as if he is close to death. We have already moved perceptibly closer to death. We are getting old. We no longer agree so readily with the opinions that we formed just yesterday. We are beginning to cherish rest, and peace, and calm, and we are annoyed when anything happens that we aren't used to. "Enthusiastic" words enthuse us less than they used to, and "profound" thoughts often seem to tax our strength beyond endurance. When we declare that something is disgraceful or shocking, our very declaration often amounts to an endorsement. The charming wonderment of a young mind, which used to be in us, has been transformed into a vague feeling of unfamiliarity towards everything. Everything is familiar to us, and we have already experienced everything; yet somehow it is hopeless, and terribly repelling. It is as if all things are still under control, yet they provoke us to irritation. We have been asked too many questions, and are now beginning to turn in upon ourselves as if threatened.

We have become unfeeling towards reality; it seems to be waiting gradually for us to bid it farewell. Our mind still works on: we read, we listen, we talk, and we try to keep on studying. These demands are tedious, but somehow we don't like to admit it. Indeed, we even have the impression that we could keep on living, and we would like to keep on living. We think that the trees we planted are perhaps just now beginning to bear good fruit, and so it would not be so easy for us to depart this life right now. But even if we were permitted to stay awhile, all this would still continue on in the same way. So it remains true: we are slowly getting old and tired. We feel as if we "still" have vigorous strength on hand, just as the afternoon is beautiful, because it is not yet evening, even though the afternoon secretly bears the evening within itself. Nothing is to be said against all this. We have neither to complain about this old age nor apologize for it. For its burden is obvious, and we are familiar with its blessing, too.

But (and this is the really alarming question of our old age), have we not also become old and tired in that "inner" man that Saint Paul speaks of? "Even though our outer man is decaying, yet our inner man is being renewed day by day" (2 Cor 4:16). Isn't our life's experience just the opposite (and this is our secret worry): though the outer man is still quite well preserved, the inner man is decaying more and more day by day. Hasn't our inner man, too, become old and tired? Doesn't our spiritual "man" disappoint us more and more?

At some time or another in the past, when we consciously set about becoming men and christians, did we not fancy that the coming life would be more beautiful, more adventurous, more fruitful?

Perhaps we once wished to become "holy"; perhaps not. In any case: even if we can now no longer bring ourselves to use this word in so carefree a manner as before, and even if a certain embarrassment creeps over us when a preacher tosses this word off so calmly, in younger days we did not think this way. The only thing that we can say is what we might have done and should have done, and what we still should do and —yes, this is just the point (may I say it softly?)—still should *will* to do. Dare I still, right now, say that we *will* it, when we were really supposed to have become it? In bygone days, we wanted to become holy. Once we desired to wear ourselves out completely for God's honor and for the kingdom of heaven, we wanted to burn our life in the ardent flame of love. And we did not become holy.

We have certainly become more holy in the years of our life that we review in memory. We have worked. And because we worked—*mirabile dictu!*—we even really forgot ourselves once in a while and loved God, and worked for his glory through what happened to us. God has so often met us in his sacraments. Why should we think that the selfishness of our heart in its secret pride is so powerful that it could plug all the cracks against the pressure of his grace? We have experienced the ups and downs of life. We have tasted its bitterness. Why should the scorching, pitiless summer have brought only aridity and not even a little fruit? Finally, hasn't God-given contrition kept the harvest of our work quite unsoiled even if the abyss of guilt once swallowed it up? No, once more we want to be simple and modest in the trials that confront us. We want to shun the secret fancies (man's ultimate pride) that our evil stubbornness could be victorious over God's gloriously strong love, which, when it will, dissolves even the obstinate insolence of the heart. We also want to let him be greater in our life than our barren heart and admit that he can reap a harvest even out of the stony field of our soul, a harvest that praises the power of his grace. We have become holier.

But we haven't become holy. Not because we haven't worked any miracles or converted any nations or directed the inexorable stream of universal history into another bed. But rather because we haven't loved God as we really should, with the whole heart and with all our strength. We cannot yet forego this duty. We cannot be satisfied with ourselves yet. Our heart doesn't love without measure and without bound as it could love and must love. It loves a little, yes; but a little in this matter is almost worse than nothing. For the heart that completely denies itself still hasn't found its master. One thing is still left; the heart must surrender itself entirely and without division.

But who will gather up this divided, disunited heart and make it sincere, so that it can surrender itself to God, all at once, without division? Alas! our poor dilapidated heart! It is so strange: it yearns a little for stronger love, and conceals a wicked annoyance at the boundless demands of love; and both of these together are covered over by a feeling of weakness and feebleness. The heart of a man who is growing old, and who did not become holy, feels like this. The heart is well disposed, but it feels too keenly its weakness. The real opportunities for unconditional, boundless love (can man want to love any other way?), the inevitable opportunities that are sent to man—not chosen by him—no longer present themselves. Did we really waste the best hours of our life, the precious opportunities for loving God? Perhaps we have not even noticed when and where they moved through our life. Are they irretrievably lost, so that we are left only with sadness? Perhaps resignation to what we are is now the best thing for us, a resignation that silently adores God, prostrate at his feet. What we could have been and have not become will then simply disappear into his fathomless will. *Ploremus coram Domini qui fecit nos*—we shall weep in the presence of the Lord who made us. Is this the answer?

But suppose we should now admit that we have refused opportunities; suppose we confess that we have neglected them; suppose we admit that we have been dull, easy-going servants? All this is fine. But if we admit this simply because it is the right thing to do, without knowing whether we are really contrite or just cowards, then we would be no better off. For even while we were admitting this we would be saddened by the knowledge that even our repentance does not truly purify the inner man, because it is only a part of what we have become over the years—old and tired and somewhat bitter in the "inner man." In this case, even our repentance would be ourselves all over again; it would be the repentance of the subdued that leaves man unchanged. Yes, that is the way it is; even life in the Holy Spirit seems to have fallen into the clutches of the mortal law of decay and of death. And if we answer, "It's not a law, but guilt," then this harshest of judgments would only help us if we could somehow get rid of this guilt. But this seems to be not only our guilt but also our punishment, and we do not quite know how to get rid of it without thereby denying the guilt.

Is there no consolation in this balance? If we only knew whether we should really seek consolation after all! Perhaps it would be better to weep quietly and without hope, not letting ourselves be consoled until the day of the Lord comes. For on that day we wretched, woebegone beggars, with our empty hands and our lazy hearts, we who do not even know whether we are worthy of pity or contempt, will find the mercy of the Lord, because his merciful love pardons boundlessly and beyond all expectations.

Is our consolation to be precisely this: plainly and honestly to admit that our wretchedness in all its bitterness is the end result of our life? We will perhaps express it thus: "Father, receive me only as one of your meanest servants, me, the lazy and stubborn servant. In your kingdom give me only the crumbs from the table. Your servant should have earned your kingdom through the sheer dazzling workings of your grace. But now my last deed, all that's left to me, is to bow down mutely before you in my darkness, the darkness of one who has squandered grace. Whatever deeds and works I could have offered you from the vessel of my heart, as my meritorious earning of your kingdom, would always have been your grace, because you alone, through the Holy Spirit, bring such works to realization. But now my heart remains almost empty; I have wasted all that you gave me. This chasm of my being praises your loftiness, and even my tears for myself give witness to the splendor of the love you wanted to send me, that I have squandered. But your servant must confess to you that there is too much yearning for you in his heart for him not to want to welcome you, with tears of joy, as your gift. Merely because he has to welcome it as a boundless gift from you is no reason for him not to want it. It is your gift, you who are love, the love that exists only in you, the love that crowns the wretched man, and—wonder of wonders —that gratefully accepts a heart just so long as it is only there, and willing to let itself be accepted, because you are the one accepting it."

Is such a confession our consolation, our sole consolation over the meager balance of our lives? Is this perhaps even *the* consolation, the genuine good fortune, the only genuine faith in the mercy of the Lord? For in each case man must once and for all leap away from himself, he must will to rely upon himself no longer, he must set himself free. Even when he boasts about the grace that actually elevated him, even this boasting is a praise of grace. And we can only do this if we have taken hold of grace in order to set it free, received it in order to pour it out as a sacrifice of praise before God, and thus to become poor. But doesn't this happen more readily, indeed doesn't it happen—for us sinners who can be poor in spirit only if we really possess nothing—only if grace is to be had in weeping because we have refused to cooperate, and in grieving because we have frivolously wasted grace? Is the spirit allotted to us except in the bitterness of being flesh, is life allotted except in the darkness of death? Isn't the balance of despondency therefore the best profit for sinners—and when weren't we sinners?

But, dear Lord, isn't this consolation too subtle, too crafty? Isn't it really the ultimate devilishness of our heart— of our heart that really believes that it sees through the bitter experience of our wretchedness and emptiness, and understands that it is just a pious game of God's love? In regard to this consolation, do we not think in the deepest abyss of our heart that God frightens us only so that his consolation may afterwards seem more blessed to us? Do we not fancy that he makes us poor only that we may afterwards find the kingdom of his grace more glorious; do we not imagine that he lets us fall into sin and the refusal of his grace only so that he may be able to try out the generosity of his love? Do we not think this way? Indeed, doesn't this consolation ultimately mean that we have secretly told ourselves: "Be reasonable, give in, repent and admit your wretchedness in order to please God, so that he may have the joy of being generous and merciful"? With this subtle, wily rhetoric of ours, haven't we lied about God's judgment and about our refusal of his grace, about our refusal that did not have to be, but that did happen, that is irremediable and is not the way to obtain God's grace?

God, have mercy on us! How mad our thinking is! How is God's grace supposed to be recognized as grace without doing violence to grace in the process? How is guilt to be acknowledged in the act of repentance, without making guilt and repentance into a secret trap, which ensnares and clutches God's grace all the more surely, the more absolutely it seems to surrender a man to the "righteous judgment of God"? Accordingly men, who are certainly all sinners, cannot decide whether they have figured out this trap, this trick that spins back and forth on the kaleidoscope of the world and of the soul, until black again becomes white.

This consolation therefore turns out to be very unconsoling. It is dangerous, and in reality it is no consolation at all. Even in the spiritual life—indeed, especially in the spiritual life—there is something like an indeterminate entry. We want to supervise and exactly determine an action in process so that we may know for sure what our manner of doing something is. We want to observe a process; and through the very act of observing the process we necessarily change it, because the observing itself is a part of the observed event. We can find no neutral viewpoint outside of the thing for our supervision. The test is itself already a deed. And we ourselves cannot determine with the certainty of a mathematical balance how it turns out. Yet it is itself an entry in the balance, and, God knows, it is the most obscure entry, because it wants to clarify everything and bring everything into order.

And this is most dangerous. Whoever desires to take hold of his consolation *and* of God's grace, spoils it. The observing of an event has a fatal influence upon the thing observed. Whoever enjoys the pleasure of his love, perverts it. Whoever consoles himself with his remorse, lets the spring of honest tears dry up. Whoever draws up a balance in order to establish with a sigh of relief that now it is clear that he has taken hold of God's grace—at least through his complete surrender before the God of grace—this man has already falsified the balance in the very process of drawing it up. Ultimately, even the heart must remain there in the body, always hidden, continually beating, but never shut off and dismantled as an airplane engine for a check up.

We wanted to take hold of ourselves, in order to make sure of what we possessed now, since there probably will not be much more added to what we already have. But it didn't succeed too well. What, then, is left for us? Nothing, except to add further entries to life's credit sheet, to the figures that God shall total up! This is the only way that real, unconditional surrender before God's grace is possible for man. Only this way, indirectly. There is nothing left to us but to sow, not to reap; to gather, not to count up what we have gathered—even the final definitive statement of the deficit would still be such a reckoning! Nothing is left for us, except to let the heart keep on doing its work: "good works." For these are the work of the heart, because in them alone the heart really possesses itself, because it forgets itself in its deeds, because it "goes out" of itself, it spends itself, and truly possesses itself only by losing itself.

So we have to pray, and not muse over how we are doing. We do not have to know exactly how well we are doing; but we do have to love. We have to perform love's deeds and offer love's sacrifices. But we dare not seek love's feelings, precisely because in this matter we never quite know what intention these feelings spring from, and for this reason they are no safeguard for us. In God's eyes it is our heart that counts; but what counts for us, what we have to depend on, is our stalwart deeds. In the performance of our deeds in bygone days we were always feeding with frightful delight upon our own dispositions and sentiments; we have wasted and soured them. That is why today, under different circumstances, we can perform our good deeds with sentiments that are not one bit purer than they were before.

The ancients, too, certainly put their dispositions into their deeds; they did not need to stand in fear of them. If we would only learn to fear our profound thoughts and our lofty sentiments! If we would only faithlessly and skeptically once again practice a little more the "ethics" of results instead of the "ethics" of feelings. If we would give a little where it hurts, and let ourselves take advantage of it. If we really forgave from the heart, and prayed at length, and even fasted once in a while. If we would hope in good works before the judgment seat of God and expect more from the rosary, even if recited merely from duty, and from the cup of cold water given to one of the least of his brethren, than from our confounded mystical sublimities or unnerving "existential anxieties"—philosophical or theological—then we would be much better off.

Are we capable of doing this? Can we maintain that this is beyond our power? Can we say that we are too old for this? If this is what God wants of us, is it not enough, and more than enough, and not, as we tend to think, too trivial? We cannot become holy, so far as I can see: but in God's name, we can become patient and pure, and unafraid before men (in spite of our inner timidity). We can become more poor in spirit, and we can kneel for a longer time in church: that we can do, if we will to do it. Our body can do that, even if the heart might not be able to. "If we will to do it"—this is no invitation to test skeptically whether we are able to will to do it. Rather it is the challenge to do it, even though it might seem that we can't; and when the good deed is done, to notice that we were, after all, quite able to do it. We are not to think back over this willing and ability with a shudder, but we should begin again today. Enthusiasm is not necessary for that. To begin today for today; that is all that is necessary. *Sufficit dies malitia sua.* Tomorrow will take care of itself. Then let the flash of God's judgment come into our life when it will. It will only be the dawn of eternal life.

And the angel of judgment shall all the more surely raise us up to the heights of heaven because of the cup of cold water, than because of our lofty reflections.

How is our balance doing now, at the end? There is the most reliable entry, the only one that puts the balance in order, the entry that makes us forget to ask about the result of the balance: carry on with the hard, customary, routine duties of the christian life of good works. Carry on! Today and tomorrow. As long as it pleases God to let you carry on. Be on the lookout a little lest you allow those rare opportunities for greater good works slip by. And as long as our good works always give us a little pain and are bitter to the heart, as long as we do the next good work, in order to forget that the first was good, then we also know that this work is not yet degenerating into external routine, and that we have not grown pharisaically hard in the doing of good, in spite of our years.

Thus the balance becomes a dropping of the balance—I forget what lies behind me. The balance becomes a running after the prize of eternal life in the bittersweet difficulties of the christian daily life.

When we run the course in this way, then we are allowed everything. In this course, we may even be permitted to draw up a balance, thankfully or contritely. When we run the course in this way, then some day even that awareness of having been chosen out for heaven, an awareness that steals softly and furtively, like a shadow, only through the heart's most secret chamber, may come over us. Delightful grace: already the tree of life is bending lower and lower, already it is beginning to sink down into God's land. Already freedom is gradually being transformed into the blessed impossibility of escaping from God's love. Already the heart senses that the battle against God's tenacious love is already lost. He is too near, and right now his love is so near that it takes away from us the fear that we, at the end, could still love something else besides just this love. When we run the course in this way, then we cannot find words glorious enough to praise the goal towards which we are hastening. For even our most clever illusions are punier than his reality, in which we will share. When we run the course in this way, then even the expectation of having spread out before us, on our last day, our whole life and all its possibilities, even the ones we neglected and refused, will not do us any harm. For in God's land there is no resignation. God will kiss all the tears from our cheeks; even the blessed tears of repentance will then not be too bitter for him. But how shall tears dry up and resignation change into laughter, if the neglected possibilities of life do not also become reality?

Let us therefore run forward, singing: it is good. *Felix culpa!* Everything is good! And for him who runs to meet God nothing is past and lost forever. God has already bestirred himself and is quite near in the impatience of that love that makes all things new. He is near! *Hodie, si vocem eius audieritis,* "Today, if you hearken to his voice . . ." Our past fickleness is the starting point of the eternal God. Glad tidings! We are running towards God—and he is already near!

IV

EPIPHANY

MOST LIKELY we have all taken part in the festivities of these
last few days of the holy Christmas season. We are merry and
gay, or perhaps, since it is not always easy to be in a festive
mood, we were only quiet and thoughtful; perhaps we were
even a little melancholy. But still, it was a break from the
routine monotony, and it did us all some good. For, in these
days devoted to children and to *the* child, our hearts have
been a little lighter and a little more responsive to the things
that lie behind mere routine.

The feast of the Epiphany, the manifestation of the Lord,
closes this festive season. It is, properly speaking, still the
feast of Christmas, that Christmas which came to the West
from the eastern part of the Church in the fourth century
A.D., and was fixed here near the Christmas feast that was
already celebrated on December 25. It is the feast of the
proclamation and manifestation of the Savior and Redeemer
to men beyond his own nation, to the "Gentiles," i.e. to all
nations and all men collectively. The message of this feast
is that the grace of our God and Savior Jesus Christ and his
love for man has appeared.

In effect, this feast speaks to us and says: "Behold, God
is present, still quiet and gentle, just as the spring remains in
the tiny seed, quiet and certain of victory, hidden under the
wintry earth, yet already more powerful than all the darkness and all the cold." Epiphany is the feast that announces:

"God is here. God has become a man. He has entered into the poverty and the narrow confines of our life. God has so loved us that he has become one of us." As a result, it is no longer doubtful how this drama that mankind plays upon the stage of its history will turn out. It is now certain that this tragedy that seemed to be so aimlessly improvised, full of blood and tears, is nevertheless a divine comedy, full of heavenly purposefulness. Now God no longer merely gazes down upon the drama, but he himself has a role to play and he himself speaks the decisive word, the key word. Epiphany—feast of the Lord's manifestation, which is still the celebration of the holy night that is brighter than our gloomy day, because it is the night that welcomed the eternal light into our darkness.

However, there is yet a *new* movement in this second Christmas feast, one that did not stand out so much in the first. Not only has God come to *us*, but in the power of this divine action man himself has come into the movement; men themselves go to him who has come to them. Indeed, one of the names we give to this feast, to this "supreme day" (as the Middle Ages called it), is "The Feast of the Three Kings." Untheological and unhistorical this cherished name for the feast may be, because the Wise Men at the crib neither constitute the subject matter of the feast, nor were they kings, nor were there, for sure, even three of them; yet the name "Three Kings" points out to us a significant aspect of the feast's mystery: that the first men searched thoroughly for the child who was their Redeemer, roving like pilgrims, journeying from afar and through every sort of danger. So this day is the feast of the blessed journey of the man who seeks God on his life's pilgrimage, the journey of the man who finds God because he seeks him. When we read of the Magi in the first twelve verses of the second chapter of Saint Matthew, we are really reading our *own* history, the history of our own pilgrimage. Led by the star, these Magi from far off Persia struggled through deserts and successfully asked their way through indifference and politics until they found the child and could worship him as the Savior-king.

It is our history that we read there. Or better: it *should* be our history. Do we not all have to admit that we are pilgrims on a journey, men who have no fixed abodes, even though we must never forget our native country? How time flies, how the days dwindle down, how we are eternally in change, how we move from place to place. Somewhere, and at some time or other, we come into existence, and already we have set out on the journey that goes on and on, and never again returns to the same place. And the journey's path moves through childhood, through youthful strength and through the maturity of age, through a few festal days and many routine weekdays. It moves through heights and through misery, through purity and through sin, through love and through disillusion. On and on it goes, irresistibly on from the morning of life to the evening of death. So irresistibly, so inexorably does it move on that we often fail to notice that we fancy ourselves to be standing still, because we are always on the move and because everything else also seems to be going along with us, everything else that we have somehow managed to include in the course of our life.

But where does the journey lead? Did we find ourselves— when we awoke to our existence—placed in a procession that goes on and on without our knowing where it is leading, so that we have only to settle down and get accustomed to this motion, learn to tolerate it, and conduct ourselves in an orderly and peaceful fashion, and not dare to consult God's will to find out where this procession is really going? Or do we actually look to find a goal on this journey, because our secret heart knows that there is such a goal, however difficult and long the road might be? Is man merely a point in the world, in whom the world's nothingness is personified?

Does our spirit glow, only to realize painfully that it emerged from the darkness of nothingness to sink back into it again, just as a shooting star glows for a moment when it travels through our atmosphere on its dark journey to the empty universe? Do we run the course only to lose the way in the end? And doesn't the heart and the mind dare inquire beforehand about the law of the road, without growing stiff in terror over the speechless, helpless shaking of the head which is the only answer? Or can't such a question be asked? But who could forbid the heart such a question?

No, we know very well that God is the goal of our pilgrimage. He dwells in the remote distance. The way to him seems to us all too far and all too hard. And what we ourselves mean when we say "God" is incomprehensible: Ground of all reality; Sea to which all the brooks of our yearning make their way; nameless "Beyond" behind all that is familiar to us; infinite Enigma that conceals all other enigmas in itself and forbids us to seek their definitive solution in what we know or in what can be experienced here on earth; boundless Immensity in purest simplicity, in actuality, truth, light and life and love. To him flows the huge stream of all creatures through all time, through every change and every succession. Doesn't our poor heart also have to set out to seek him? The free spirit finds only what it looks for. And God has promised in his word that he lets himself be found by those who seek him. In grace he wills to be not merely the one who is always a little farther beyond every place that the creature on pilgrimage has reached, but rather to be that one who really can be found, eye to eye, heart to heart, by that small creature with the eternal heart whom we call man.

Behold, the wise men have set out. For their heart was on pilgrimage towards God when their feet pointed towards Bethlehem. They sought him; but he was already leading them because they sought him. They are the type of those who yearn for salvation, yearn in hunger and thirst for righteousness. That is why they did not think that man could dare omit his one step just because God has to take a thousand in order for both to meet. They were looking for him, for salvation, in the heavens and in their heart. They sought him in seclusion and among men, even in the holy writings of the Jews. They see a strange star rise in the heavens. And God in his blessed kindness even allows their astrology, foolish though it may be, to succeed this once, because their pure hearts did not know any better.

Their hearts must have trembled a little when the theory drawn from their obscure knowledge of the Jewish expectation of salvation and from their astrology should now suddenly become applied in practice in a very concrete journey. Their bold hearts must have been a little frightened. They would almost have preferred that their hearts not take quite so seriously the noble principles of the theoretical reason, principles so foreign to reality and so unpractical. But the heart is strong and courageous. They obeyed their hearts, and they set out.

And suddenly, just as they leave their native land behind them, at the moment when they dared to take the leap into a hazardous venture, their hearts become light, like the heart of one who has ventured all and is more courageous than is really possible—according to everyday proverbs. They travel over tortuous paths, but in God's eyes their path led straight to him because they sought him in sincerity. It frightened them to be so far from their familiar native country, but they knew that in journeying everything has to be transformed, and they marched on and on in order to find *the* native land that will be more than a tent by the wayside. They knew from their own deeds (life is more than the mind's theories) that to live means that we are always changing, and that perfection means passing through many levels of change.

So they journeyed. The way was long and their feet were often tired, their hearts often heavy and vexed. And it was a strange, painful feeling for their poor hearts to have to be so entirely different from the hearts of other men, who, engrossed in their everyday affairs with such perfect stupidity, looked with pity at these travellers walking past on a journey that was so uselessly squandering their hearts. But their hearts carry on to the end. They do not even know where the courage and strength keep coming from. It is not from themselves, and it just suffices; but it never fails as long as one does not ask and does not peer inquisitively into the empty reaches of the heart to see if something is inside, but bravely keeps on spending the mysterious contents of the heart. Their hearts cannot be intimidated. They do not look arrogantly upon the men whom they pass. But they do move past them, and think, "He shall also call these men, when it pleases him to do so. But we dare not be disloyal to the light, just because it does not yet seem to shine for them."

From the scribes in Jerusalem they got sullen information; and a cunning commission from a king. But from these sources their ears heard only a heavenly message, because their hearts were good and were full of yearning. And when they came and knelt down, they only did what they had in reality always been doing, what they were already doing during their search and journey: they brought before the face of the invisible God now made visible the gold of their love, the incense of their reverence and the myrrh of their suffering. Then their path led out from the land of salvation history. They disappear from our horizon as quietly as they came (like those who die). But whoever has once poured out his whole heart for the star, to the very last drop, has already encountered the adventure of his life in that single instant. These men, who have disappeared from our horizon, had royal hearts. If their real journey continued on to the invisible, eternal light—indeed, if it really began only when they returned to their own country—then such royal hearts found their definitive home. And that is why we want to call them by that joyous name of days gone by: the holy kings from the East.

Let us also step forth on the adventurous journey of the heart to God! Let us run! Let us forget what lies behind us. The whole future lies open to us. Every possibility of life is still open, because we can still find God, still find more. Nothingness is over and done with for him who runs to meet God, the God whose smallest reality is greater than our boldest illusion, the God who is eternal youth and in whose country there dwells no resignation. We roam through the wilderness. Heart, despair not over the sight of the pilgrimage of mankind, the pilgrimage of men who, stooped over with the burden of their suppressed terror, march on and on, everyone, so it seems, with the same aimlessness. Do not despair. The star is there and it shines. The holy books tell where the Redeemer is to be found. Ardent restlessness urges us on. Speak to yourself! Doesn't the star stand still in the firmament of your heart? It is small? It is far away? But it is there! It is small only because you still have so far to go! It is far away only because your generosity is thought capable of an infinite journey. But the star is there! Even the *yearning* of the inner man for freedom, for goodness, for bliss, even the *regret* that we are weak, sinful men—these, too, are stars. Why do you yourself push clouds in front of the star— the clouds of bad temper, of disappointment, of bitterness, of refusal, clouds of sneering or of giving up—because your dreams and expectations have not been realized?

Throw down your defences! The star is shining! Whether or not you make it the lode-star of your journey, it stands in your sky, and even your defiance and your weakness do not extinguish it. Why shouldn't we, then, believe and go on the journey? Why shouldn't we look to the star in the firmament of our hearts? Why not follow the light? Because there are men like the scribes in Jerusalem, who know the way to Bethlehem and do not go there? Because there are kings like Herod, for whom such news of the Messias only means inconvenience for their political plans, kings who even today make an attempt on the child's life? Because most men remain sitting at home with the sullen worldly-wisdom of their narrow hearts, and consider such adventurous journeys of the heart as nonsense? Let us leave them and follow the star of the heart!

How shall I set out? The *heart* must bestir itself! The praying, yearning, shy but honest heart, the heart well-versed in good works sets out, and journeys towards God. The heart that believes and does not become soured, the heart that considers the folly of goodness to be more sensible than the cunning of egoism, the heart that believes in God's goodness, the heart that will lovingly let its guilt be forgiven by God (this is harder to do than you may think), and that lets itself be convinced by God of its secret unbeliefs—that is not surprised at this, but gives glory to God and confesses— such a heart has set out towards God on the adventurous journey of a royal heart.

A new year has begun. During this year, too, all the paths from east to west, from morning 'till evening, lead on and on as far as the eye can see, through the deserts of life, with all its changes. But these paths can be turned into the blessed pilgrimage to the Absolute, the journey to God. Set out, my heart, take up the journey! The star shines. You can't take much with you on the journey. And you will lose much on the way. Let it go. Gold of love, incense of yearning, myrrh of suffering—these you certainly have with you. He shall accept them. And we shall find him.

V

SHROVE TUESDAY

CAN THE subject of our reflection for Shrove Tuesday be anything but laughter?*

We do not mean the sublime heavenly joy that is the fruit of the Holy Spirit, nor the joy that "spiritual men" like to talk about in soft, gentle terms (a joy that can easily produce a somewhat insipid and sour effect, like the euphoria of a harmless, balanced, but essentially stunted person). No, we mean real laughter, resounding laughter, the kind that makes a man double over and slap his thigh, the kind that brings tears to the eyes; the laughter that accompanies spicy jokes, the laughter that reflects the fact that man is no doubt somewhat childlike and childish. We mean the laughter that is not very pensive, the laughter that ceremonious people (passionately keen on their dignity) righteously take amiss in themselves and in others. This is the laughter we mean. Is it possible for us to reflect on this laughter? Yes, indeed, very much so. Even laughable matters are very serious. Their seriousness, however, dawns only on the man who takes them for what they are: laughable.

Is laughter such as we mean proper even to a spiritual man? Naturally, if it doesn't suit us, we should not toil over it. Such laughter must come from the heart—yes, from that

* Translator's note: The celebration of the *Festnacht* (principally in southern Germany) is equivalent to the festivities known as Mardi Gras or Carnival.

49

heart that not even the saint is complete master of. In order to be a spiritual man, then, one does not need to force this laughter when it doesn't come of itself. We do not doubt the spiritual worth of someone who doesn't laugh in this way. By no means. The question is only this: whether or not the spiritual man must rightly call this laughter into question, whether or not he has to attack it as incompatible with the dignity of a spiritual man. No! Not at all! Let us explain and justify this laughter. When we do so, laughter shall smilingly tell us very serious things.

In the most pessimistic book of the Bible we read: "There is a time to weep and a time to laugh; a time to mourn and a time to dance" (Eccl 3:4). This is what laughter tells us first of all: there is a time for everything. Man has no fixed dwelling place on this earth, not even in the inner life of the heart and mind. Life means change. Laughter tells us that if as men of the earth we wanted to be always in the same fixed state of mind and heart, if we wanted always to brew a uniform mixture out of every virtue and disposition of the soul (a mixture that would always and everywhere be just right), laughter tells us that fundamentally this would be a denial of the fact that we are created beings. To want to escape from the atmospheric conditions of the soul—the human soul that can soar as high as the heavens in joy and be depressed down to death in grief—to want to escape by running under the never-changing sky of imperturbability and insensitiveness: this would be inhuman. It would be stoical, but it would not be christian. This is what laughter tells us first of all.

It speaks to us and says, "You are a man, you change, and you are changed, changed without being consulted and at a moment's notice. Your status is the inconstancy of trans-formation. Your lot is to stop and rest at no one status. You are that manifold, incalculable being that never factors out without a remainder. The being that can be broken down into no common denominator other than that which is called God—which you are not, and never will be. Woe to you if, while immersed in time, you should want to be the never-changing, the eternal; you would be nothing but death, a dried up, withered man.

"Laugh with me," says laughter. "But not all the time! Always and everywhere I want to be quite little, like God's great and noble creatures. Only the laughter of hellish despair should be continual on this earth. Only the devils should laugh like this, not you. But laugh sometimes, and laugh with ease. Do not be afraid of laughing a little stupidly and a little superficially. In the right spot this superficiality is deeper than your toiling thoughtfulness, which was suggested only by a spiritual pride, a pride that does not want to endure being a mere man. There really is a time for laughter; there has to be, because this time, too, is created by God. I, laughter, this little childish simpleton who turns somersaults and laughs tears, I am created by God.

"You cannot encircle and capture me. You cannot put me down on your spiritual budget in so many precisely figured columns, like nickels, dimes, and pennies. It is hard to prove that, according to God's will and according to the principles of ascetical and mystical theology, I am supposed to crop up, to turn my somersaults just where I please. But for all that, I am one of God's creatures. Let me into your life, then. Don't worry, you won't lose anything by letting me in. The fact that you shall still weep and be sad takes good care of that worry."

Laugh. For this laughter is an acknowledgment that you are a man, an acknowledgment that is itself the beginning of an acknowledgment of God. For how else is man to acknowledge God except through admitting in his life and by means of his life that he himself is not God but a creature that has his times—a time to weep and a time to laugh, and the one is not the other. A praising of God is what laughter is, because it lets man be man.

But it is more, this harmless laughter. True, there is a laughter of fools and of sinners, as the wise Sirach instructs us (21:20; 27:13), a laughter which the Lord cursed in his woes (Lk 6:25). Naturally, we do not mean this laughter: the evil, unhappy, desolate laughter which seeks to help us escape the incomprehensibility of history by trying to comprehend this drama of history as a cruel, silly trick, instead of revering it as a divine comedy, serene and confident that its meaning will one day be clear to us.

We are thinking here of that redeeming laughter that springs from a childlike and serene heart. It can exist only in one who is not a "heathen," but who like Christ (Heb 4:15; cf. 1 Pt 3:8) has thorough love for all and each, the free, detached "sympathy" that can accept and see everything as it is: the great greatly, the small smally, the serious seriously, the laughable with a laugh. Because all these exist, because there are great and small, high and low, sublime and ridiculous, serious and comical, because God wills these to exist—that is why this should be recognized, that is why everything should not be taken as being the same, that is why the comical and the ridiculous should be laughed at. But the only one who can do this is the man who does not adapt everything to himself, the man who is free from self, and who like Christ can "sympathize" with everything; the man who possesses that mysterious sympathy with each and every thing, and before whom each can get a chance to have its say.

But only the man who loves has this sympathy. And so laughter is a sign of love. Unsympathetic people (people who cannot actively "sympathize" and who thus become passively unsympathetic as well) cannot really laugh. They

cannot admit that not everything is momentous and significant. They always like to be important and they occupy
themselves only with what is momentous. They are anxious
about their dignity, they worry about it; they do not love,
and that is why they do not even laugh. But we want to
laugh and we are not ashamed to laugh. For it is a manifestation of the love of all things in God. Laughter is a praise of
God, because it lets man be a loving man.

But it is more, this harmless, innocent laughter of the
children of God. All that is fleeting is an image, even the
pleasant and rather casual laughter of everyday life. And in
this case we do not even need to discover the likeness. The
word of God himself has declared the real analogies. Scripture
accepts this laughter that almost always borders on the
trivial. Laughter, not merely a smile. Laughter, not merely
joy and confidence. And Scripture makes this small creature
(which, of course, will have to grow dumb and dissolve into
nothingness when it treads the halls of eternity) into a picture
and likeness of God's own sentiments. So much so that we
would almost be afraid to attribute to God the harsh, bitter,
scornful laughter of pride. The thrones in heaven laugh
(Ps 2:4). The Almighty laughs at the wicked man, for he sees
his day already approaching (36:13). Wisdom, speaking of
the ungodly, tells us that the Lord shall laugh them to scorn
(4: 18).

God laughs. He laughs the laughter of the carefree, the
confident, the unthreatened. He laughs the laughter of divine
superiority over all the horrible confusion of universal
history that is full of blood and torture and insanity and
baseness. God laughs. *Our* God laughs; he laughs deliberately;
one might almost say that he laughs gloatingly over mis-
fortunes and is aloof from it all. He laughs sympathetically
and knowingly, almost as if he was enjoying the tearful drama
of this earth (he can do this, for he himself wept with the

earth, and he, crushed even to death and abandoned by God, felt the shock of terror). He laughs, says Scripture, and thus it tells us that an image and a reflection of the triumphant, glorious God of history and of eternity still shines in the final laugh that somewhere springs out from a good heart, bright as silver and pure, over some stupidity of this world. Laughter is praise of God because it is a gentle echo of God's laughter, of the laughter that pronounces judgment on all history.

But it is still more, this harmless laughter of the loving heart. In the beatitudes according to Luke (6:21), this is what we find: "Blessed are you who weep now, you shall laugh!" Of course, this laughter is promised to those who weep, who carry the cross, those who are hated and persecuted for the sake of the Son of Man. But it is *laughter* that is promised to them as a blessed reward, and we now have to direct our attention to that point. Laughter is promised, not merely a gentle blessedness; an exultation or a joy that wrings from the heart tears of a surprising happiness. All this, too. But also laughter. Not only will our tears be dried up; not only will the great joy of our poor heart, which can hardly believe in eternal joy, overflow even to intoxication; no, not only this—we shall laugh! Laugh almost like the thrones; laugh, as was predicted of the righteous (Ps 51:8).

It is a most awful mystery, this laughter of finality, this laughter which will accompany the saved as they depart this drama of universal history, this laughter that on high will be the ultimate (as incessant weeping in the depths), when stage and auditorium of universal history have become empty forever.

But you shall laugh. Thus it is written. And because God's Word also had recourse to human words in order to express what shall one day be when all shall have been—that is why a mystery of eternity also lies deeply hidden, but real, in everyday life; that is why the laughter of daily life announces and shows that a man is on good terms with reality, even in advance of that all-powerful and eternal consent in which the saved will one day say their "Amen" to everything that he has done and allowed to happen. Laughter is praise of God because it foretells the eternal praise of God at the end of time, when those who must weep here on earth shall laugh.

The 17th, 18th, and 21st chapters of Genesis tell a strange story, the story of Abraham and his wife: how he became the father of all believers in receiving the promise of a son, because he believed, against all hope, in God who makes the dead live and calls into being that which does not exist (Rom 4). In the telling of this promise and its fulfillment, it is also said that the father of all believers and his wife—she who in her hopeless old age bore him his son, from whom Christ is descended—laughed (Gn 17:17; 18:12-15; 21:6). Abraham threw himself on his face and laughed. Sarah laughed to herself. "God has made me a laughing stock," she says, when she had borne the son of promise. The laughter of unbelief, of despair, and of scorn, and the laughter of believing happiness are here uncannily juxtaposed, so that before the fulfillment of the promise, one hardly knows whether belief or unbelief is laughing.

Fools laugh, and so do wise men; despairing non-believers laugh, and so do believers. But we want to laugh in these days. And *our* laughter should praise God. It should praise him because it acknowledges that we are men. It should praise him because it acknowledges that we are loving men. It should praise him because it is a reflection and image of the laughter of God himself. It should praise him because it is the promise of laughter that is promised to us as victory in the judgment. God gave us laughter; we should admit this and—laugh.

VI

ASH WEDNESDAY

Shrove Tuesday is over. There is a time to laugh and a time to weep (Eccl 3:4). Now we hear the words, "Remember, man, that you are dust, and unto dust you shall return." With the dust of the earth the priest traces on our foreheads the sign of the cross, the sign of the Son of Man, so that what we are in reality may be made perceptible in sign: men of death and men of redemption.

Dust is a good subject for reflection on Ash Wednesday, for dust, the symbol of nothingness, can tell us a great deal.

The prayer that accompanies the distribution of ashes comes from Genesis (3:19), where the divine judgment is pronounced over all men, who had become sinners in their first parents. The divine judgment falls dark and hopeless over men: "From the earth you were taken; dust you are and to dust you shall return."

We dare not introduce into this text our platonic outlook on life, and think, "Oh fine, man's body is clearly declared to be mortal. But what of it, for the soul is certainly immortal, and it can find no fault with this death, which in the long run isn't so bad." On the contrary, this text, this judgment is directed to the whole man: "*You* are dust." Dust is an image of the whole man. We may subsequently modify this image by distinguishing a twofold meaning: one meaning for man's body and one for his soul. Even in this distinction, however—which is certainly justified in itself—we stick to the one compact statement of Scripture only when we do not forget that the assertion made in Genesis is concerned first of all with the whole man; and that this one assertion contains everything that pertains to man, body and soul, even if it does so in different ways. *Man*, therefore, and not just a part of his essence, is dust.

Understood in this way, dust is naturally an image, a graphic symbol. But it is an image that is fuller and deeper than our metaphysical ideas, which are often so remote and diluted. What, then, does this image tell us about man?

The symbol of dust was used as a declaration of man's essence not only in Genesis. "God is mindful that man is only dust" (Ps 102:14). In Ecclesiastes 3:20 we read, "All are from the dust and all return to the dust." Pessimistic? Yes, but this must be endured so that the joyous message of the New Covenant can be grasped. Even pessimism can be inspired by God. In the book of Job (4:19), the despondent Eliphaz complains in these words, "How we who dwell in houses of clay, whose foundation is in the dust, are crushed like the moth." "I am merely dust and ashes," says Abraham to God, in order to move him to pity for a sinful race (Gn 18:27). And if man's death is to be described, Coheleth again has recourse to the image: "the caper berry bursts, the silver cord is snapped, the golden bowl broken, the pitcher shattered at the spring, the broken pulley falls into the well—and the dust returns to the earth, just as it was . . . : *vanitas vanitatum, omnia vanitas*" (Eccl 12:5–8).

Dust—truly a splendid symbol. Dust, this is the image of the commonplace. There is always more than enough of it. One fleck is as good as the next. Dust is the image of anonymity: one fleck is like the next, and all are nameless.

It is the symbol of indifference: what does it matter whether it is this dust or that dust? It is all the same. Dust is the symbol of nothingness: because it lies around so loosely, it is easily stirred up, it blows around blindly, is stepped upon and crushed—and nobody notices. It is a nothing that is just enough to be—a nothing. Dust is the symbol of coming to nothing: it has no content, no form, no shape; it blows away, the empty, indifferent, colorless, aimless, unstable booty of senseless change, to be found everywhere, and nowhere at home.

But God speaks to man: "You are dust." You—the whole of you—are dust. He does not say that man is only dust. It is an existential expression, not a complete formula of man's essence. It can be spoken, though, even by itself, because the truth that it expresses must be experienced and endured to the full, so that whatever further is to be said about man (and there is a lot more, indeed everything, left to be said), this first assertion is not denied, watered down, nor essentially restricted. For it lies in a completely different dimension. Man is not a little dust and also at the same time and in the same dimension, still a lot more, so that to be a creature of dust would not be so bad. Rather, he is *all* dust, and is more than dust only when he really admits this dust-existence, accepts it, and "endures through it" with body and soul. And because it is a question of an existential formula in this sense, then Scripture can address this formula to man plainly, in all its harshness. Scripture need not add the comforting thought that man is more than dust, because this added notion, spoken in the wrong place, would be no comfort at all. Rather it would be the temptation not to take this dust-existence seriously, but to deceive oneself about it.

Truly, then, Scripture is right. Man is dust. He is always in the process of dying. He is the being that sets its course for death, when it sets out on life's journey, and steers for death, clearly and inexorably. He is the only being that knows about this tendency to death. He is dust!

To be sure, he is spirit, too. But left to its own resources, what is the spiritual existence except the knowledge of things incomprehensible, the knowledge of guilt, and the knowledge that there is no way out of all this. Man has enough spirit in him to know God. But what does this mean except that he knows he stands before an unfathomable being whose ways are unsearchable and whose judgments are incomprehensible? What does this mean except that he stands before the Holy One as a lost sinner; what does this mean except that with his mind he grasps the meaning of what he is in reality: dust and ashes?

Perhaps this dust might want to boast that it is immortal spirit. If so, what would this boast mean except that this dust is, by its very nature, subject to the judgment, that as a sinner this dust has already been judged? What else would it proclaim by this boasting of its eternity except that it is dust, nothing but the commonplace, nothing but the abnormality of guilty indebtedness, nothing but anonymous insignificance, nothing but nothingness? Taken by itself, what is the spirit except the possibility of measuring the finite with an infinite norm, only to perceive with horror that the eternal cannot be reached.

And so through his practical experience man comes to realize that he is dust. Scripture tells us that man is like the grass of the field, an empty puff of air. Man is a creature of pain and sin and of drifting perplexity, who is constantly and continually losing his way in blind alleys. Man tortures himself and others, because he does not know whether guilt comes from pain or pain from guilt. Despair is always threatening man, and all his optimism is only a means of numbing his hopeless, bleak anxiety. Dust, that is what man is.

It is not easy for man to avoid hating himself (as Bernanos tells us). Actually, if dust really belongs to man, is really a part of him, then we shouldn't hate it. That is why men of the orient, keenly aware of their origins, had such a remarkable relationship with dust, man's proper image. He strews dust on his head, weeping and lamenting (Jos 7:6; 1 Sam 4:12; 2 Sam 1:2; Job 2:12; La 2:10). In tears he throws himself down and sits in the dust for which he was made (Is 47:1). The reason why we cast our enemy down into the dust, tread on him in the dust, and make him eat the dust, is because the proud hatred and triumph over an enemy really flares up in white heat at its own despair over itself (Is 25:12; 26:5; Jos 10:24; Ps 109:1; Mich 7:10; Ps 71:9; Is 49:23). What we hate in others is ourselves; we cannot stand someone else because we despair in our own selves as seen in others.

Dust doubtlessly has an inner relationship, if not an essential identity, with another concept of both Old and New Testaments: the concept of "flesh." "Flesh" certainly designates, in both testaments, the *whole* man. It designates the whole man precisely in his basic otherness to God, in his frailty, in his intellectual and moral weakness, in his separation from God, which is manifested in sin and death. The two assertions, "man is dust" and "man is flesh," are, then, more or less essentially similar assertions.

From this conclusion, however, we must now go on to understand the change that the sentence "man is dust" undergoes in the christian economy of salvation. The good news of salvation rings out: "The Word became flesh." St. Paul said that God sent his own Son in the likeness of human, sinful flesh (Rom 8:3). We can add to this and say that God himself has strewn his own head with the dust of the earth, that he fell on his face upon the earth, which with evil greed drank up his tears and his blood. Even more, we can say to him exactly what is said to us, yes, we can tell the eternal God: "Remember, man, that you are dust, and in death you shall return to dust." We can tell him what he told us in Paradise, because he has become what we are after Paradise. He has become flesh, flesh that suffers even unto death, transitory, fleeting, unstable dust.

But ever since then, as Tertullian says, this *caro* has become the *cardo salutis*. Flesh has become the hinge, the pivot of salvation. Since then, flesh designates not only the pivot and hinge of the movement into nothingness and death, but also the pivot and hinge of a movement that passes through dust's nothingness and forlornness into life, into eternity, into God.

Ever since that moment, the sentence of terrifying judgment, "dust you are," is changed for the man of faith and love. This is not the man who despairs at the downward movement of returning into the dust, and who "puts on the brakes" because he wants to stop this movement short of anxiety and terror. Rather, the man of faith and love is the man who causes the movement to swing further, right into the midst of the dust and through it. This judgment still has a mysterious and shocking sense. The old sense is not abolished. The old sense must be endured and experienced in tears, in the experience of nothingness and of death, in evil and in dying, in the bitterness of internal and external limitations.

But even this existential sense of the pronouncement that man is dust contains another depth. The downward motion of the believer, the descent with Christ into the dust of the earth, has become an upward motion, an ascent above the highest heaven. Christianity does not set free from the flesh and dust, nor does it bypass flesh and dust; it goes right through flesh and dust. And that is why the expression "dust you are" is still applicable to us; rightly understood, it is a complete expression of our life.

Tomorrow morning when we hear the words, "Remember, you are dust," we are also told then that we are brothers of the incarnate Lord. In these words we are told everything that we are: nothingness that is filled with eternity; death that teems with life; futility that redeems; dust that is God's life forever.

To say this is easy. To endure it is hard. But we have to endure it. In the boredom of everyday routine, in the disappointments that we experience in everything—in ourselves, in our neighbors, in the Church—in the anxiety of time, in the futility of our labor, in the brutal harshness of universal history. Again and again we shall lie in the dust of our weakness, humiliated and weeping (grant, God, that this image shall never be realized in all its reality: in these days, a grave of atomic dust is all too possible). We shall experience again and again that we are dust. We shall not only be told this in a ceremony; but we shall experience it in life, and throughout life.

Just as the dying in baptism is only the beginning of a life-long dying into the death of Christ, so too, the cross of ashes is only the renewed beginning of the return movement into the dust. Just as the sacrament of baptism is an image and symbol of the approaching humble reality of routine everyday life and of the splendor and glory hidden therein, so too, the sacramental is an image and a symbol of the approaching humble reality of everyday life, and of the splendor and glory hidden therein.

VII

LENT

DOES IT not seem strange that even today the Church dedicates a special season to penance? We can easily understand that men of earlier centuries may have required such a season for the housekeeping of their spiritual and religious life: they were gay, content, and carefree men, whose heartfelt laughter rang out as they celebrated *mardi gras* in the streets. That is why they could experience—so we like to think—a short season of composure, of reflective seriousness, and of ascetical checking of their zest for living, and feel this only as a pleasant change in the tides of their life and of their soul.

But for us? Don't we feel that the Church's proclamation of the season of seriousness, of contemplation, and of fasting is strangely at cross-purposes with reality? Doesn't a season of fasting seem to us almost like a ceremony from the good old days, a ceremony that comes to us with a light covering of dust? What meaning, what purpose does such a season have today for men who are suffering want, who are past all earthly hopes and are bitter at heart—men who would gladly fast, if they weren't already starving?

No, for us the season of fasting begins long before Ash Wednesday, and it will also continue far beyond the forty days until Easter. It is so real that we need not utilize this Lenten season—now permanently fixed in the liturgical year —like a conveniently available stage prop for our feelings.

The non-liturgical season of fasting of our present-day life seems to us even harder and more bitter than some of the painful times of a past race. For we suffer not only from lacking the contentment and the carefree security of life, not only from sitting in darkness and in the shadow of death, but above all—dare we be bold to say how it really is?—we suffer because *God* seems to be far from us.

God is far from us. This is not a statement that applies to everyone. It is not a statement that should alarm the God-filled heart. But it is also not a statement in which the person to whom it applies dare take pride, thinking that at least the bitterness of his heart is infinite. This is not a statement that trumpets forth a characteristic that man should ignore, a characteristic that would seem to prohibit God from bestowing his nearness and the certainty of his blessed love, as if despair makes a man's heart greater than good fortune does. To make the distance of God into the proud nobility of man (as do many forms of that interpretation of life called existential philosophy) is sin, at once stupid and perverse. In many people, God's distance is simply a fact that is there and that demands an explanation. It is a pain, the deepest pain of the fasting season of life, the season that lasts as long as we travel as pilgrims, far from the Lord.

God's "distance" here does not mean that a man denies the existence of God or that he ignores God's existence in his own life. This may often—but by no means always—be a false reaction to the situation that we mean. Here God's distance means something that can be found just as well—indeed, even above all—in believing men, in men who yearn for God, in men who gaze out towards his light and the gladness that his nearness brings. Even these persons (yes, especially these) can and must often experience what we mean: to them God seems most unreal—he is mute and silent in refusal, as if he embraces our existence only as an empty, distant horizon would embrace it; our thoughts and the demands of our heart go astray in this pathless infinity and wander around, never to find their way out. God's distance means that our spirit has become humble in the face of an insoluble puzzle. It means that our heart is despondent over unanswered prayers, and is tempted to look on "God" only as one of those grand and ultimately unbelieved-in words under cover of which men hide their despair, because this despair no longer has the power to accept even itself as real. God seems to us to be only that unreal, inaccessible infinity which, to our torment, makes our tiny bit of reality seem still more finite and questionable. This infinity makes us seem homeless even in *our* world, because it leads us to the extravagance of a yearning that we can never fulfill, and that even he does not seem to fulfill.

Yes, it appears that Western mankind of today, more than the men of earlier times, must mature expiatingly in the purgatory of this distance from God. If in the destiny of individuals it happens that besides the blessed day of the near God, there is the night of the senses and of the spirit, in which the infinity of the living God comes nearer to men by seeming to be more distant and not at all near, why should such times not also be experienced in the destiny of nations and continents? Why shouldn't this, in some way and in some measure, be the holy lot of all? (That the blame for such a condition belongs, perhaps, to one particular era, is no proof against the fact that this condition can be a *felix culpa*.) Seen from this point of view, the declared atheism of many people, theoretical as well as practical, would then be only the false reaction to such an event—false, because impatient and mistaken. It would be reactionary in the proper sense: it clung to the childish experience of the near God as claim and condition of worshipping acknowledgment. When that childish experience is gone, then a man can no longer start with God, and there is nothing for him. The atheism of our day, then, would be the stubborn blocking off of the self against calling out in the dark purgatory of a choked-up heart for the God who is always greater than the God thought of and loved the day before.

Enough. There is a distance of God that permeates the pious and the impious, that perplexes the mind and unspeakably terrifies the heart. The pious do not like to admit it, because they suppose that such a thing should not happen to them (although their Lord himself cried out, "My God, my God, why have you forsaken me?"); and the others, the impious, draw false consequences from the admitted facts.

If this God-distance of choked-up hearts is the ultimate bitterness of the fasting season of our *life*, then it is fitting to ask how we are to deal with it, and (for us it is the very same question) how we can today celebrate the fasting season of the *Church*. For when the bitter God-distance becomes a divine service, the fasting season of the world changes into the fasting season of the Church.

The first thing we have to do is this: stand up and face this God-distance of a choked-up heart. We have to resist the desire to run away from it either in pious or in worldly business. We have to endure it without the narcotic of the world, without the narcotic of sin or of obstinate despair. What God is really far away from you in this emptiness of the heart? Not the true and living God; for he is precisely the intangible God, the nameless God; and that is why he can really be the God of your measureless heart. Distant from you is only a God who does not exist: a tangible God, a God of man's small thoughts and his cheap, timid feelings, a God of earthly security, a God whose concern is that the children don't cry and that philanthropy doesn't fall into disillusion, a very venerable—idol! That is what has become distant.

Should one not endure such a God-distance as this? Indeed,

we can truly say: in this experience of the heart, let yourself
seemingly accept with calm every despair. Let despair fill
your heart so that there no longer seems to remain an exit
to life, to fulfillment, to space and to God. In despair, despair
not. Let yourself accept everything; in reality it is only an
acceptance of the finite and the futile. And no matter how
wonderful and great it may have been, let it be really you;
your own self, you with your ideals, you with the preliminary
estimate of your life (which was sketched out and planned
with such shrewd precision), you with your image of God,
that satisfies *you* instead of the incomprehensible One
himself. Make *yourself* block up every exit; only the exits to
the finite, the paths that lead to what is really trackless, will
be dammed up. Do not be frightened over the loneliness and
abandonment of your interior dungeon, which seems to be so
dead—like a grave. For if you stand firm, if you do not run
from despair, if in despair over the idols which up to now you
called God you do not despair in the true God, if you thus
stand firm—this is already a wonder of grace—then you will
suddenly perceive that your grave-dungeon only blocks the
futile finiteness; you will become aware that your deadly void
is only the breadth of God's intimacy, that the silence is filled
up by a word without words, by the one who is above all
name and is all in all. That silence is God's silence. It tells
you that he is there.

   That is the *second* thing you should do in your despair:
notice that God is there. Know with faith that he is with you.
Perceive that for a long time now he has been waiting for you
in the deepest dungeon of your blocked-up heart, and that
for a long time he has been quietly listening to you, even
though you, after all the busy noise that we call our life, do
not even let him get a word in edgewise, and his words to the
man-you-were-until-now seem only deadly silence. You shall
see that you by no means make a mistake if you give up you

anxiety over yourself and your life, that you by no means make a mistake if you relax your hold on self, that you are by no means crushed with despair if once and for all you despair of yourself, of your wisdom and strength, and of the false image of God that is snatched away from you.

As if by a miracle, which must be renewed every day, you will perceive that you are with him. You will suddenly experience that your God-distance is in truth only the disappearance of the world before the dawning of God in your soul, and that the darkness is nothing but God's brightness, that throws no shadow, and your *lack of outlets* is only the immeasurability of God, to whom no road is needed, because he is already there. You shall see that you should not try to run away from your empty heart, because he is already there, and so there can be no reason for you to flee from this blessed despair into consolation that would be no consolation, into a consolation that does not exist. He is there. Do not seek to hold him fast. He does not run away. Do not seek to make sure of yourself and to touch him with the hands of your greedy heart. You would only be clutching at a straw, not because he is distant and unreal, but because he is the Infinite who cannot be touched. He is there, right in the midst of your choked-up heart, he alone. But he is all, and so it appears as if he were nothing.

If we do this, then peace comes all by itself. Peace is the most genuine activity: the silence that is filled with God's word, the trust that is no longer afraid, the sureness that no longer needs to be assured, and the strength that is powerful in weakness—it is, then, the life that rises through death. There is nothing more in us then but God; God and the almost imperceptible and yet all-filling faith that he is there, and that we are.

But one thing more must still be said: this God-distance would not be the rising of God in mortal, choked-up hearts if the Son of Man, who is the Son of the Father, had not suffered and done just this with us and for us and on our behalf in his own heart. But he has suffered and done all this. It happened in the garden, from whose fruit men wanted to press out the oil of joy, the garden that was in truth the garden of the lost paradise. He lay on his face; death crept into his living heart, into the heart of the world. Heaven was locked up and the world was like a monstrous grave; and he alone in that grave, choked up by the guilt and helplessness of the world. As refreshment, the angel who looked like death passed him the cup of bitterness, that he might sink into agony. The earth wickedly and greedily gulped down the drops of blood of his mortal terror. God blanketed everything as with a night that no longer promised day. One can no longer separate him from death. In this vast death-silence—men slept, dulled by grief—in this death-silence the small voice of the Son floated somewhere, the only sign from God that was still left. Each moment it seemed to be stifled. But a great miracle took place: the voice remained. The Son spoke to the awful God with this tiny voice that was like a dead man's, "Father"—he spoke to his own abandonment—"Thy will be done." And in ineffable courage he commended his abandoned soul into the hands of this Father.

Ever since that moment, our poor soul, too, is laid in the hands of this God, this Father, whose former decree of death has now become love. Ever since that time, our despair is redeemed, the emptiness of our heart has become fulfillment, and God-distance has become our homeland. *If* we pray with the Son, and, in the weary darkness of our heart, repeat his prayer in the garden. In pure faith. No storm of rapture will spring up, when his words mysteriously rise up somewhere in the depths of our hearts as our own words. But their strength will suffice. For each day it will be just enough. So long as it pleases God. And this is enough. He knows when and where our heart will be sufficiently purified—only here on earth can it be purified—to endure also the dazzling dawn of his blessedness. Our poor heart, that now in faith in Jesus Christ shares with him the night, which to the believer is nothing other than the darkness of God's boundless light, the darkness that dazzles our eyes, the heavenly night, when God is really born in our hearts.

All of this cannot be simply a religious poem for Sunday thoughts. It must be practiced in the burden and bitterness of daily life. If you begin to practice it, to stand firm and willingly drink the cup that contains poverty and want and God-distance, a blessed fasting season begins for you. Will you try it? Speak to the nearby God of your heart and say, "Give me your grace that I may do it."

VIII

ST. JOSEPH

THE CATHOLIC Church today celebrates the feast of her
patron, her heavenly protector. We can understand such a
feast only if we believe in the Communion of Saints, if we
know by faith that God is not a God of the dead, but a God
of the living, if we confess that whoever has died in God's
grace lives with God and precisely for that reason is close to
us, and if we are convinced that these citizens of heaven
intercede for their brothers on earth in the eternal liturgy of
heaven.

The meaning of such a feast can be grasped only if we
believe that after death all the events of this earthly life are
not simply gone and past, over and done with forever, but
that they are preparatory steps that belong to us for eternity,
that belong to us as our living future. For our mortality does
not change to eternity in an instant; rather, it is slowly
transformed into life.

The blessed men with whom we have fellowship in the
Communion of Saints are not pale shadows. Rather, they
have brought over into the eternal life of God the fruits of
their earthly life, and thus have brought with them their own
personal uniqueness.

Their God even calls them by name in the one today of
eternity. They are ever the same as they were in the unique
history of their own lives. We single out one individual from
among them to honor him as our heavenly protector and

intercessor, because his own individuality means something unique and irreplaceable to us. We mean that between him and us there exists a specific rapport that makes him a special blessing for us and assigns a special duty to us, if we are to be worthy of his protection.

From this point of view, is it possible to think that Joseph, the spouse of the Blessed Virgin and foster father of our Lord, is particularly suited to be a patron of twentieth century man? Is it possible to think that anyone living today will be able to see himself reflected in Joseph? Are there not people today who, if they are true to their character as willed by God, are a people of small means, of hard work, of only a few words, of loyalty of heart and simple sincerity? Certainly every christian and every christian nation is charged with the entire fullness of christian perfection as a duty that is never completed. But every nation and every man has, so to speak, his own door, his own approach, through which he alone can come nearer to the fullness of christianity. Not all of us will find access to the boundless vistas of God's world through the great gate of surging rapture and burning ardor. Some must go through the small gate of quiet loyalty and the ordinary, exact performance of duty. And it is this fact, I am inclined to think, that can help us to discover a rapport between earth and heaven, between christians today and their heavenly intercessor.

The pages of the Bible tell us little about Joseph. But they tell us enough to know something of our heavenly patron. Not a single word of his has been recorded for us. He pondered, yes; that is expressly attested to. But he spoke little, so little that these words did not have to be transmitted to posterity. We know that he was a descendant of the noble lineage of David, the greatest in his nation's history. But that was the past that the present, in its sober poverty, had yet to make perceptible. This present, however, was the hard life of one insignificant carpenter in a tiny village in one corner of the world. For the poor this present meant paying taxes and standing in line. It was the destiny of the "displaced person," who had to seek scanty shelter among strangers, until the political situation again permitted a return to his homeland, the homeland that he must have loved, since he renounced living in the neighborhood of the capital city and stayed in the "province" country of Galilee. He lived very inconspicuously in his Nazareth, so that the life of his family furnished no spectacular background for the public appearance of Jesus (Lk 4:22). However, this humble routine of the life of an insignificant man concealed something else: the silent performance of duty.

Three times the Scripture says of Joseph: "He rose up." He rose up to carry out God's will as he perceived it in his conscience, a conscience that was so alert that it perceived the message of the angel even in sleep, although that message called him to a path of duty that he himself neither devised nor expected.

According to the witness of the Bible, this insignificant man's humble routine concealed a further object of value: righteousness. Joseph was a just man, the Bible says, a man who regulated his life according to the Word and Law of God. Not only when this law suited his desires, but always and at all times, even when it was hard, and when the law judged to his disadvantage that his neighbor was right. He was righteous in that he was impartial, tactful, and respectful of Mary's individuality and even of that which he could not understand in her.

This loyalty to duty and impartial righteousness, which is a manly form of love, also lived in him with respect to God his Father. He was a devout man and he was manly in his devotion. For him the service of God was not a matter of pious feelings that come and go, but a matter of humble loyalty that really served God and not his own pious ego. As Luke says: "Every year he went to Jerusalem for the Passover feast, according to the custom." Now we can tell what was the most important element in the life of this man whose everyday life was a life of duty, of righteousness and of manly devotion: this life was given the charge of protecting in a fatherly way the Savior of the world.

He received into his family the One who came to redeem his nation from their sin, One to whom he himself gave the name of Jesus, a name which means "Yahweh is Salvation." Silent and loyal, he served the eternal Word of the Father, the Word who had become a child of this world. And men called their Redeemer the son of a carpenter. When the eternal Word was audible in the world in the message of the gospels, Joseph, having quietly done his duty, went away without any notice on the part of this world.

But the life of this insignificant man did have significance; it had one meaning that, in the long run, counts in each man's life: God and his incarnate grace. To him it could be said: "Good and faithful servant, enter into the joy of your Lord." Who can doubt that this man is a good patron for us? This man of humble, everyday routine, this man of silent performance of duty, of honest righteousness and of manly piety, this man who was charged with protecting the grace of God in its embodied life?

Christians of today might find their way back to what is best in them if the individuality of this man, their patron, were again producing more stature in them. Granted, a nation must have greatness of spirit and pioneers who will lead her towards new goals. Just as much, if not more so, however, a nation needs men and women of life-long performance of duty, of clear-headed loyalty, of discipline of heart and body. A nation needs men who know that true greatness is achieved only in selfless service to the greater and holy duty that is imposed upon each life; men of genuine reverence, conquerors of themselves, who hear the word of God and carry out the inflexible decrees of conscience. It needs men who through their lives bear the childlike, defenseless grace of God past all those who, like Herod, attempt to kill this grace. A nation needs men who do not lose confidence in God's grace, even when they have to seek it as lost, as Joseph once sought the divine child. Such men are urgently needed in every situation and in every class.

We have a good patron, who is suitable for everyone. For he is a patron of the poor, a patron of workingmen, a patron of exiles, a model for worshippers, an exemplar of the pure discipline of the heart, a prototype of fathers who protect in their children the Son of the Father. Joseph, who himself experienced death, is also the patron of the dying, standing at our bedside. We have inherited from our Father a good patron. But the question put to us is whether we remain worthy of this inheritance, whether we preserve and increase the mysterious rapport between us and our heavenly intercessor.

Joseph lives. He may seem far away from us, but he is not. For the Communion of Saints is near and the seeming distance is only appearance. The saints may seem eclipsed by the dazzling brightness of the eternal God, into which they have entered, like those who have vanished into the distance of lost centuries. God, however, is not a God of the dead, but of the living. He is the God of those who live forever in heaven, where they reap the fruits of their life on earth, the life that only seems to be past, over and done with forever. Their earthly life bore *eternal* fruit, and they have planted that fruit in the true soil of life, out of which all generations live.

And so Joseph lives. He is our patron. We, however, will experience the blessing of his protection if we, with God's grace, open our heart and our life to his spirit and the quiet power of his intercession.

IX

GOOD FRIDAY

ONE PART of the Good Friday liturgy of the Church is the unveiling of the cross. The priest unveils a large cross, and kneeling down sings the following words three times: "Behold the wood of the cross, on which hung the Savior of the world; come, let us adore!"

What takes place in the simple power of liturgical gesture is only a shadowy image of what actually happened and is happening in the history of mankind. The cross of Christ has cast its shadow over all time. To be sure, historically speaking, the cross was erected only once in a definite place—on that hill of execution near the gate to the city of Jerusalem; and at a definite time—in the year 33, under the Emperor Tiberius. And it was all over in three short hours. And then, no more.

But all time had waited for this moment that seems so short. All that had gone before flowed together into this moment. It was the hidden meaning and goal of all the long centuries that passed before the event of the Cross. The ages of the early fathers, of the patriarchs and of all races were impregnated, darkly and in a concealed way, by the power of this event. Invisibly and without notice, but directed by the hidden wisdom of the Lord of all history, all roads led to this place, all the roads that men, weeping and with bloody feet, had traveled since the first day of mankind's history, usually without knowing where they led. All the events of universal history could only ripen to their hidden fruit that is eternity, when this event took place in the fullness of time. If, previous to Christ's coming, people went astray, then it was because they did not know the one terminus of time, the Cross, which alone remains while everything else changes. When they went the right way, then it was because they were already being led by that power that draws all men to the One who is lifted up on the cross.

Yes, the ages before Christ were overshadowed by the Cross. They were mysteriously mapped out to be a part of that divine and universal drama of the history of mankind, in which the cross of Christ, the glorification of the Lord on the cross, is the deciding word.

However, what was already mysteriously at work in the heart of these ages was concealed from them just as the ultimate meaning, the ultimate importance and the real impression produced by a word that we ourselves speak is only really revealed when a response comes back to us from some other quarter. But before the word was actually spoken from the cross, no one knew what answer God would give to all the words of human history, to the cries of guilt and of need, of yearning and of complaint, and of urgent petition. Before the Cross, no one knew definitively and unequivocally what God would say to man.

Now, however, God has spoken his final word in this world and in its history, the word that is the Cross of his Son. And in the two thousand years since the Cross, men have been advancing in a never ending, drab procession to meet this unveiled Cross—whether they knew it or not—in all the tangles and meaningless twistings of their path through life. Yet they have been advancing with a formidable resoluteness towards this unveiled Cross. Men from the beginning of their history, and of their misfortune, had been marching towards it, always in the dark shadow of the veiled cross. And in the two thousand years since the crucifixion, what came to pass during those three hours—when the Cross on Golgotha pierced the heavens and the Man thrust out upon it died— what took place then, happens again and again, continually. Many pass by, and many remain.

Many pass by. Their glance lights by chance upon him who hangs on this gibbet. Then they hurry on. For they will have nothing to do with such a one. To help is impossible. Even to stay there demands being well-disposed. All things considered, it comes down to this one person, the Crucified. That's that. And you can't make a man who is nailed to the cross into the world's turning point. No one need seriously consider that. Many pass by. Perhaps they glance back and take one final look; they shake their heads, they laugh, they blaspheme. They may even be saddened; in any case, they proceed to their daily agenda, declaring that Bacchus is a better symbol of the meaning of life than Christ crucified. They pass by, perhaps white with hate for the crucified, who will ostensibly rob them of the pleasure of life. They pass by regretfully, perhaps, like Cleophas: "But we had hoped that he would redeem Israel and now it's already the third day." Many pass by. On and on. Am I among those who pass by? Who pass by the truth of life, pass by God, pass by the true salvation? Am I in the procession that flows past the cross and spills into the darkness? Even those who wear christian garments and who use christian gestures, even pious christians can hasten past the cross of Christ. Past, until all is past. Many pass by the unveiled cross.

Many remain. Because they belong there. Because here they have found everything. They stay. They kneel down. They kiss the scars. Sinners—we are all sinners—kneel down before this cross. For we have crucified him. Because our sins were laid upon him. Death is born from our sins, the death that overpowered him. He suffered from the sins we have committed. Sinners kiss the wounds that they themselves have caused. The murderers flee from their guilt to the murdered One, the executioners to their own victim. And so I go to him. And sinners, who themselves are crucified with him on the cross of their own guilt, speak: "Lord, think of me when you come into your kingdom."

The dying lie at his feet. For they suffer *his* destiny. They die because he died. True, everyone must die because of sin. But God has allowed this deadly guilt in his kingdom of this world for a reason. He held this world embraced in his love for his incarnate Son, in whose death he was so able to overcome sin through greater grace that the world could not escape his mercy. And therefore death, which we ourselves caused and which we suffer as the wages of sin, is first, last, and always only the death that causes the death of sin.

Those who suffer weep before his cross. What night of need was not his night? What fears are not sanctified by his? To be raised up in hope, what grief needs to know more than that it has been borne by the Son of Man, who is the Son of God?

Before him the children kneel. For he has loved them, and although he knew what is in each person, he relied on them and threatened with his woe whoever scandalized one of these little ones.

Before him kneel the old people, who—let us be honest— have nothing more in sight and can count on nothing but to die. They kneel before their dying God. And they know that the greatest grace and hardest act of their lives are still to come. Only the man who dies in him and with him receives this grace rightly and carries out the act perfectly.

Before him kneel the homeless, and they gaze upon him who willed to die abandoned by his own people, outside the city near the highway, after living a hard life, not knowing where he would lay his head, poorer than the foxes, who have their dens.

The lonely kneel silently before him. For, as he was dying, the loneliest man of all, he knew them in the solitude of death and of abandonment by God. And he allowed all their bitter loneliness into his own heart, until everything else was driven out, except love for the abandoned.

Widows and mothers who have lost their sons kneel before him, weeping. For his eyes still look lovingly and with concern through the dark shadows of death that surround him, upon the mother whom he must leave lonely.

Lovers prostrate themselves before the crucified. For with him is all the strength of love and all the strength that turns the disillusion of love into that love which is stronger than death, into that unique love of Christ that can feed on its own fire and stay alive.

Before the cross the scholars and wise men of this world kneel. They learn thereby that all wisdom that does not burn in the blessed foolishness of love is vain; they learn thereby that the logic of the cross, which to the Greeks is folly and to the Jews a scandal, is God's wisdom and God's strength for those who are saved by it. And they learn that it has pleased God to save the world through the folly of the cross, before which every mouth is dumb and all the wisdom of the world humbles itself—before the folly of divine love.

God's priests kneel before the cross, because they have to preach the cross and they are always drinking from the chalice of his failure. They kneel there because, with their sins and weakness, they are always putting themselves between God's light and men, because more than all others they need his mercy. The account demanded of them shall be whether they prized the blood that today flowed from the wounds of the Son of Man.

It is also possible for those who think they cannot believe to remain standing there and to look at him. If they are humble men who long for the light, and if they do not run away from the light in their greatest need—and today there are many like this—then they are such that suffer with Christ without knowing it. They should look upon the One who, as he was dying, cried out, "My God, my God, why have you forsaken me?" They should have the courage to love as their brother the One who (since he was the eternal Son of the Father) came into the dim, deadly darkness, in which a man has God only in the complete abandonment of everything, even of himself. They should recognize their night as part of the Son's Good Friday. If they have dismissed from their hearts the impression that God is dead, then—if they only grasp it with faith—they share God's destiny of death, who himself willed really to die for them, who willed to be dead so that they might live and believe that even the furthest distance can be outreached by the silent love of their God.

Before his Cross "I" kneel. Do you kneel there, solitary, ineffable ego that does not even know itself, that is a wavering spark between the abyss of nothingness and the abyss of eternity? If I do not know myself and my origin, if my destiny is hidden from me, if I stand in fear before myself and before the chasms of my heart—where should I stay, if not before the Cross, in which the incomprehensibility of man's destiny becomes the revelation that God is truly love. I kneel before him. And I am silent. For what shall I tell him, except what I am? And if I have never understood myself, what else can I do except surrender myself to him completely, to him whose love, loyal even to death, alone has understood me? And if this ego silently loves and lovingly commits itself, then it perceives that it finds its true essence and its genuine likeness precisely in the Crucified.

So all who have come to know the mercy of God kneel before the cross that invisibly towers up through all space and all time. They prostrate themselves. They are silent.

They weep. They adore the Crucified. They adore the life that was given for us. They adore the death that brought us life. They adore the love that loved to the end, the obedience that was strong to the point of death, even to death on a cross. They adore the mystery that contained the answer to all questions. They look on him whom they have pierced and they understand the sins that they have committed, and the righteousness which the Son has satisfied, and the justice which came over sinners as mercy. They gaze at him who forevermore stretches his hands out towards a stubborn and rebellious people. They want to be close to the Son of the Father, close to their dead brother who sacrificed himself for them. They want to be close to the one door through which the path leads into God's freedom, away from the slavery of finiteness and from the shame of sin. They want to possess him who alone proves that God loves to the end, the sole proof that by itself prevails against the thousand judgments of God that seem to testify to his wrath. They attend to the pledge that has value even in God's sight. They tend the sacrifice that alone penetrates through all heaven. They praise the consolation of their weary soul and the strength of their weak heart. They want to hear him who, in the torment of his agony, prayed for his enemies; who, in the shadow of death, thought of his friends; who promised Paradise as he died; who committed his soul into the hands of the Father. They want to hear him who can say that he fulfilled all things. They see with anxiety that he is no longer veiled from them, for they know, when they see their naked crucified Lord, that they are looking at the end result of all sin and all agony. For only light and happiness can come after this, the lowest depths of all calamity and terror.

They wait—if necessary, for a lifetime—until he, with lips that burn from thirst, also speaks a word to them. Let it sound as it will, it is a word of his mercy and of his love.

This is enough. So those who are redeemed, those who weep and those who love, kneel under the Cross of the world.

Do I kneel thus below the Cross for the three hours of my life, until everything is also fulfilled in me and through me? Am I one with the Crucified? My soul thirsts for God my Savior. I want to rise up and I want to see him who has drunk the most bitter cup of this world. The most bitter, for in comparison what is the little bitterness that we feel, we who are sinners and so indifferent to it all? I want to kiss his bloody feet, the feet that pursued me even into the most monstrous inextricability of my sins. I want to see the pierced side of him who has locked me in his heart and who therefore took me with him when he went home, passing over from this world through death to the Father, so that I, too, am now there where only God can be. I want to see the wood of the Cross, on which the salvation of the world, my salvation, hung. Come let us adore him.

X

EASTER

To do justice to the mystery of Easter joy with the stale words of human speech is rather difficult. This is so not only because every mystery of the Gospel penetrates only with difficulty into the narrow confines of human life—thereby making it even harder for our words to grasp and contain and express these mysteries—but because the Easter-message is the most human tidings of christianity. That is why we find it the most difficult message to understand. For what is most true, most obvious, and most easy, is the most difficult to be, to do, and to believe. That is to say, modern man bases his life on the unexpressed, and therefore all the more self-evident, prejudice that anything "religious" is merely an affair of the most interior heart and of the loftiest spirit—something that we must bring about by ourselves, something, therefore, that involves the difficulties and unreality of the heart's thoughts and moods.

But Easter tells us that God has done something. God himself. And his action has not merely gently touched the heart of a man here and there, so that they tremble slightly from an ineffable and nameless someone. God has raised his Son from the dead. God has quickened the flesh. God has conquered death. He has done this—he has conquered—not merely in the realm of inwardness, in the realm of thought, but in the realm where we, the glory of the human mind notwithstanding, are most really ourselves: in the actuality of this world, far from all "mere" thoughts and "mere" sentiments. He has conquered in the realm where we experience practically what we are in essence: children of the earth, who die.

Children of the earth—that is what we are. Our existence is caught up in birth and death, in the body and in the earth, in bread and in wine. The earth, in short, is our home. Of course the fine, delicate, perceiving mind that looks to the eternal, and the soul that gives life to everything, these two must be blended into this earthliness like a mysterious "essence of spirit" if it is to be all worthwhile and authentic. But the mind and the soul must be in the realm where we exist: on earth and in the body. They must be there as the eternal splendor of earthly beings. They cannot be there simply in the sense of a pilgrim who, like a misunderstood foreigner, roams phantom-like over the stage of the world in one short episode. We are children of this earth; we are too much a part of the earth to wish to take our leave from her once and for all.

It is true enough that for the earth to be bearable, heaven itself must be bestowed on us. Yet heaven must bow down and stand over this abiding earth as a blessed light; heaven must break forth in splendor from the dark womb of the earth.

We belong to this earth. But if it is impossible for us to be disloyal to the earth—not from any self-will or self-mastery, which does not befit the sons of the humble-earnest mother earth, but because we must be what we are—then we are mortally sick with a mysterious illness that sticks fast in the innermost part of our earthly being. Our great mother, the earth, is herself afflicted. She groans under the burden of transitoriness. Her happiest feast is suddenly like the beginning of a funeral. And when we hear her laugh, we tremble with fear lest in the next moment she weep beneath her laughter. She bears children who die; they are too weak to live forever, and yet they have too much spirit to relinquish eternal joy without a fight, because, unlike the beasts of the earth, they see the end before it is upon them, and they are not compassionately spared the fully conscious experience of that end. The earth bears children of infinite hearts, and, alas, what she gives them is too beautiful for them to scorn, and too poor to satisfy them fully, for they are insatiable.

Earth is the region of this unfortunate gap between the grand promise that does not set free and the scanty gift that does not liberate. And that is why she also becomes the rich plentiful soil of sin, as her children try to tear away from her more than she can rightly give. She may cry out that she herself was rent asunder in just this way by the original sin of the first man of the earth, whom we call Adam. But this changes nothing. Right now she is that hapless mother: too keenly alive and too beautiful to be able to send her children away from her so that they might win for themselves in a different world a new homeland, a homeland of eternal life; too poor to give them the fulfillment of that yearning which she gives them. And she brings forth both life and death, not one without the other, because she is always both, and never one nor the other. And we call this muddy mixture of life and death, of joy and sorrow, of creative activity and tedious duties—we call this our everyday life.

Here we are on the earth, our homeland forever; and yet, this does not suffice. This adventure to escape from what is earthly does not spring from cowardice, but from loyalty to our own nature. What are we to do? Listen to the good news of the resurrection of the Lord! Is Christ the Lord risen from the dead, or not? We believe in his resurrection, and therefore we confess that he died, that he descended into the kingdom of the dead, and that he rose on the third day. But what is the significance of all this and why is it a blessing for the children of the earth?

The incarnate Son of the Father has died; he who is the eternal fullness of divinity, the necessary, the boundless, the holy One, who is the Word of the Father even before time exists, and who is at the same time the child of this earth, the Son of the blessed Mother—this One has died. This is therefore the death of one who is at one and the same time the Son of God's fullness and the child of earth's indigence. But death does not mean—as we myopically suppose like the quite un-christian spiritualists—that his mind and his soul, the vessel of his eternal divinity, have wrenched themselves away from the world and the earth, and flown to God's vast splendor beyond the world. Death does not mean that his soul has escaped, simply because the body, which held it down to the earth, is broken in death, and because the murderous earth has shown that the child of everlasting light could find no homeland in her darkness.

"Was crucified, died, and was buried," we say, and to that we immediately add, "he descended into the lower regions and he rose from the dead." With this addition, "died" takes on a meaning entirely different from the notion of escaping from the world, the sense we are accustomed to give to death. Jesus himself said that he would descend into the heart of the world (Mt 12:40), into the heart of all earthly things where everything is linked together and is one, where death and futility hold sway in the midst of this consolidation. Down into death he has penetrated. He let himself be conquered by death—holy stratagem of eternal life—so that death would gulp him down into the innermost depths of the world. In this way, having descended to the very womb of the earth, to the radical unity of the world, he could give the earth his divine life forever.

Because he died, he belongs all the more to the earth. For when the body of a man is embedded in its grave of earth, the man (his soul, we say), even though in God's immediate presence after death, enters all the more into definitive unity with that one mysterious basis in which all spatial and temporal things are linked together, and the soul lives on, as from its root. By this death the Lord has descended into this lowest depth. Now he is there; futility and death are there no longer. In death he has become the heart of this earthly world, the divine heart in the innermost heart of the world. And here the earth, "behind" her continual development in space and time, sinks her root into the power of the all-mighty God.

Christ has risen from this one heart of all earthly things where realized unity and nothingness were no longer distinguishable. He has not risen for the purpose of departing once and for all from that heart of the world. He has not risen so that the travail of death which brings him forth anew might so bestow upon him God's life and light that he would leave behind him the dark womb of the earth, hopelessly barren. He has risen in his *body*. And this means that he has already begun to transform the world into himself. He has forever taken the world to himself; he is born anew as a child of this earth. But it is now an earth that is transfigured, an earth that is set free, that is untwisted, an earth that is established forever in him and that is forever redeemed from death and from futility. He rose, not to show that he had forsaken the grave of the earth, but to prove that he has definitively transformed even this grave of death—body and earth— into the glorious, immeasurable dwelling of the living God and of the God-filled soul of the Son.

The risen Lord has not moved out from earth's little hut. For, as a matter of fact, he still has his body—in a definitive and glorified state, yes, but still his body. It is a part of this earth that belongs to the earth forever as a share of her reality and her destiny. He has risen in order to reveal that through his death the life of freedom and of bliss remains forever rooted in earth's narrow confines and in her grief, in the very center of her heart.

What we call his resurrection—and unthinkingly take to be his own private destiny—is only the first surface indication that all reality, behind what we usually call experience (which we consider so important), has already changed in the really decisive depth of things. His resurrection is like the first eruption of a volcano which shows that God's fire already burns in the innermost depths of the earth, and that everything shall be brought to a holy glow in his light. He rose to show that this has already begun. The new creation has already started, the new power of a transfigured earth is already being formed from the world's innermost heart, into which Christ descended by dying. Futility, sin and death are already conquered in the innermost realm of all reality, and only the "little while" (which we call history "A.D.") is needed until what has actually already happened appears everywhere in glory, and not only in the body of Jesus.

Because he did not begin to heal, to save, and to transfigure the world by transfiguring the symptoms on the surface, but began rather at the innermost root, we suppose that nothing has happened to the essence beneath this superficial area. Because the waters of grief and guilt still flow on the surface where we stand, we fancy that their source in the depths is not yet dried up. Because evil still carves new marks in the face of the earth, we conclude that in the deepest heart of reality love is dead. But these are only appearances, which we take for the reality of life.

Christ is risen because in death he conquered, and redeemed forever, the innermost center of all earthly existence. And, having risen, he has kept this innermost center in his control, and he continues to preserve it. If we acknowledge that he has gone away to God's heaven, this is only another way of saying that he withdraws from us for a while the tangibility of his transfigured humanity. But this is only another way of saying that there is no longer any abyss between God and the world.

Christ is already in the midst of the poor things of this earth—the earth which we cannot leave because she is our mother. He is in the ineffable yearning of all creatures who, without knowing it, yearn for a share in the transfiguration of his body. He is in the history of the earth, whose blind course, with all its victories and all its crashing defeats, steers with uncanny precision towards the day when his splendor, transforming everything, will erupt out of the earth's own depths. He is in all the tears as hidden joy, and in every death as the life that conquers by seeming to die. He is in the beggar, to whom we give a coin, as the secret rich reward that returns to the giver. He is in the miserable defeats of his servants as the victory that belongs to God alone. He is in our weakness as the strength that dares to let itself seem weak, because it is invincible. He himself is even right in the midst of sin as the mercy of everlasting life that is prepared to be patient to the end. He is present as the mysterious law and the innermost essence of all things—the law that triumphs and succeeds even when all order seems to be crumbling. He is with us like the light and air of day, which we do not notice; like the mysterious law of a motion that we do not grasp, because the segment of this motion that we ourselves experience is too short for a formula to be educed by us. But he is there. He is the heart of this earthly world and the mysterious seal of its eternal validity.

That is why we children of the earth may love the earth; that is why we must love her, even when she terrifies us and makes us tremble with her misery and her destiny of death. For ever since Christ, through his death and resurrection, penetrated the earth for all time, her misery has become provisional and a mere test of our faith in her innermost mystery, which is the risen One himself. Our experience does not tell us that he is the mysterious meaning of her misery; by no means! It is our faith that tells us this. The faith that offers blessed consolation to all that we experience in life, the faith that can love the earth because she is, or is in the process of becoming, the "body" of the risen One. We do not need to leave her, for the life of God dwells in her. When we want both the God of infinity (how can we help wanting him?) and the familiar earth, as it is and as it shall become, when we want both for our eternally free homeland, there is *one* path to *both!* For in the resurrection of the Lord, God has shown that he has accepted the earth for all time. *Caro cardo salutis*, said one of the Fathers of the Church in an untranslatable play on words: the flesh is the hinge of salvation.

The hereafter to every exigency of sin and of death is not somewhere in the life hereafter; it has come down to us and lives in the innermost reality of our flesh. The most sublime religiosity of seclusion from the world would not fetch the God of our life and the salvation of this earth from the distance of his eternity; and it would not even reach him in his world. But he himself has come to us. And he has transformed what we are and what we still want to consider as the gloomy, earthly dwelling place of our "spiritual nature": he has transformed *the flesh*. Ever since that event, mother earth bears nothing but transformed children. For his resurrection is the beginning of the resurrection of all flesh.

One thing, of course, is necessary for his event—which we can never undo—to become the blessedness of our existence: he must burst forth from the grave of our hearts. He must rise from the core of our being, where he is as power and promise. He is there, and yet something remains to be done. He is there, yet it is still Holy Saturday, and it will continue to be Holy Saturday until the last day, until that day that will be the cosmic Easter. And this rising takes place beneath the freedom of our faith. It is taking place as an event of living faith that draws us into the colossal eruption of all earthly reality into its own glorification, the splendid transfiguration that has already begun with the resurrection of Christ.

XI

ASCENSION

HE HAS departed from us. It is alarming that we feel no grief. He must have intended that we be consoled; but our barren and shallow hearts are astonished at this kind of comfort. First of all, we must reflect for a long time before we begin to grasp the fact that we are supposed to be inconsolable over his going away. Yes, it is true: to be comforted, we actually would have had to detain him here on earth.

A shocking fear of the emptiness that he left behind must have come over us. At last there was in our midst someone who was not superfluous; someone who did not *become* a burden, but who *bore* the burden. Because he was good, so unassumingly good, we almost took it for granted! Someone who gave a name to the incomprehensible puzzle behind all things—he called it his "Father"—and did so with neither incredible naiveté, nor with tasteless presumption. Indeed, he almost led the world into the temptation of taking it for granted, when he allowed us, too, to whisper into the divine darkness, "Our Father." It was God's mercy and his eternal Wisdom in our midst.

At last, we were able to imagine something about God besides the abstractions of philosophers. At last, there was someone who knew something, and yet did not have to speak with clever eloquence. Someone we needed only to touch, someone we dared to kiss. Someone we slapped on the shoulder in a friendly way, and he did not get all upset about it. And in these trivialities we had everything—everything incarnate: we had God, his mercy, his grace and his nearness. The eternal Word of the Father had compressed himself into our flesh. Oh, that he did not shudder at this incomprehensibly foolish undertaking—to make God's life a resident in the stall of this world.

And now he is gone away again, and we accept it with indifference. Perhaps we secretly imagine that he could not stand it in our midst. Naturally not, when they crucified him. Dear God, I surely would have done it too, had I been there. Can I (just as I am right now) seriously consider myself better than they? I would be absolutely forsaken, if Christ had not prayed for his enemies, and so for me. That's the only consolation, the only certainty. For only those who are lost are unaware of this consolation. Can a person like me believe in you and love you? I hope so, Lord. Have mercy on me!

Or did he put up with it all and endure it even to the extent that he has taken up to heaven what he assumed in the Incarnation? Actually, it would not have been good for us if he had stayed behind here on earth. For even we cannot endure it here forever. Yes, we die. Somewhere, and in some manner, some of us even willingly. We die either from despair or from yearning after freedom: we choose either the death of death or the death of life. But to stay here forever! That would be the wandering Jew in eternal hell.

It was therefore right, quite right, for him to go away. He certainly did what could be done here on earth (pardon me, what only *he* could do here). For the sake of this earth, in boundless love for this terrible earth—did he confuse it with his Father, or is this confusion precisely his mystery, justified because the Father gave it to him?—for the sake of this earth, he let his heart be pressed out to the last drop, like a grape. He let all his heart's fullness flow down into this earth. Greedily the earth swallowed it up, until the fire of guilt and terror in her innards was quenched, and her inmost cavity was filled up with the blood of God himself. He did what he could do here. It was not his affair that the Father, in his kindness, did not let the earth burst into flames immediately. That was his Father's business. He was pleased that *we* should still have something to say and do. Christ himself insisted on this delay for "a little while." What bold courage! What a trusting heart! He had to go away; there was nothing more for him to do. For everything was fulfilled ever since he turned the dark night of Golgotha into the bright shining day of his love. Afterwards, he whispered swiftly to his intimate friends that this is the way to triumph. (Lord, help my unbelief!)

He has taken away with him what he had assumed, the frail flesh, the trembling heart, the human mind (which in the death-pang blacks out and knows no more answers). What I am, he assumed: this cramped hovel, full of darkness, where questions and the failure to really understand slink around like squealing rats and find no exit. Naturally, I am aware that one can talk about him with more elegant, more pleasing words if man is looked at from God's point of view. You who are irritated at this anthropology, are you just as keenly aware that you, too, are actually judging man from God's perspective: and he saw that all was good? Or do you live the light-hearted life of wood-lice, who so easily tolerate themselves? Why do you still want God, if you already think that you yourselves are so respectable?

Let us not quibble about this. Your faith and my faith firmly establish that human nature is misunderstood, if it does not as soon as possible attain to God once and for all. Such a "nature" the Son has possessed, *consubstantialis nobis*. And precisely because this nature belonged entirely to God he was aware (really aware, as an individual) of man's natural state, as long as this nature did not run away from itself into God and seek to be completely dissolved in God and absorbed in the divine nature.

This nature of ours the Son has assumed, and he has taken it with him. He has taken it to that place where we might have thought that nature must completely dissolve into nothingness, if it wants to venture the step across to the beyond. He has taken it to the only place where it can be, if it is not to find its hell right here. I need no fashionable explanation or de-mythologizing to know that I cannot imagine human nature's behavior "there," or what it does "there." I am not so spiritualistic that I find it easier to imagine a "soul" there than a body. How ridiculous are those christians who fancy that they can think of Mary in heaven with only her soul, rather than complete with body and soul. In this regard, the few Catholic "heretics" of today who put everyone who dies in God's grace in heaven with body and soul would be more correct than these others.

Therefore, I do not suppose that I can picture in my imagination a finite spirit that endures in the presence of God himself—precisely there and only there. But I do know that under pain of eternal damnation we are forbidden to be less demanding and to strive after a more modest place of happiness, or to renounce completely an eternal existence. And I do not know what a body does there. I do not know what both body and soul do there for the length of an eternity. Of course, God is eternally meaningful. But how about us? How about us with bodies and souls (or however it may be depicted)? Here on earth we do not last for very long, and we cannot imagine the beyond. Or is, perchance, the *visio beatifica*, the perception of God, no longer an absolute mystery in our faith? And have you already taken the trouble to picture in your mind exactly what a glorified body is?

And so my faith and my consolation are centered on this:

that he has taken with him everything that is ours. He has ascended and he sits at the right hand of the Father. "I see the Son of Man standing at the right hand of God." The absolute Logos shall look at me in eternity with the face of a man. Those who theorize on the beatific vision forget this. As yet, I have read nothing about this in any modern tract in dogma. How strange! At this point pious ascetics read into the silence of the dogmaticians some sentimental anthropomorphism about joy. And what is more, they even dare—on their way to the beatific vision—to bypass the humanity of Jesus. As though we can do this so casually! Whoever "imagines" things this way obviously is not sufficiently aware that God's revelation was a man.

Jesus has taken with him what he was, and what we are, to such an extent that he himself, Jesus of Nazareth, abides forever. We must be more important than we thought, of more permanent value and of more substance, when we consider that this is feasible in spite of our foolish or despairing pride. One could reduce all christianity to this one formula: it is the faith in which God so surpassed the pride of men that man's grossest imaginings of his own worth are degraded to sinful disbelief and almost brutish timidity. Moreover, when a person indulges in "pantheistic" imaginings about God's existence, on closer inspection he certainly does not make himself into God, but rather God into himself. Pantheism is no objection against what has been said above, for what does the incarnation, what does grace and glory mean except that man can endure in the midst of God, in the midst of this absolute fire, in the midst of this incomprehensibility. He can endure directly before one who is so exalted above everything that is outside of him that it is simply inexpressible? This is, nevertheless, the most unlikely truth. And it is celebrated in Christ's ascension. For in his ascension this truth has been definitively realized.

He has taken ourselves with him. No wonder, then, that

we can imagine nothing concerning this, that we today can picture less about this than the ancients could. They had Christ ascending to *caelum empyreum*. In the world of their physical science they had a place for heaven, and they had it, presumably, *even before heaven (as it really is) came to be: by means of Easter and the Ascension*. Nor is this surprising. The break-up of the picture the ancients had of the physical universe was fundamentally a very christian occurrence. Although understandable and unavoidable, the ancient notion was fundamentally very unchristian, because it made heaven exist before and independently of Christ and the events of his death and resurrection. In this view, moreover, Christ was the gate-opener of heaven rather than its founder. Whoever wants to take the *aperuisti credentibus regna caelorum*, "you have *opened* the kingdom of heaven for the faithful," so literally that Christ has done nothing except open heaven, would say too little about him. *Condidisti . . .*, "you have *established . . . ,*" would be more accurate.

Space controlled time and history. And all of this was not so christian that we today must de-mythologize merely because formerly this was not correct. For today, since the world and even space itself are seen to be finite, there is "room" enough even for a corporeal heaven, even though this can no longer be thought of (as with the ancients) as an ultimately homogeneous piece of our space, nor as an upper border on the edge of our space. And if this quite modern natural science is a unique focusing of the thought of the unimaginable on matter, we shall also learn anew to "think" of heaven simply as bodily glorification, and thus we shall learn to take seriously its reality.

The ontology of the beatific vision was indeed a very abstract matter, and we can still learn something about it from the ancients. Their gift to us is not obscurity, and indeed they believed, and knew with faith. It would not, then, be at all "modern," but worse than the ancient way, if we were to act as if we could not take the ascension (his and ours) seriously, simply because we could not picture it in our imagination.

Is he far away from us because he has ascended above the heavens? When is someone close to us? When we can touch him and kiss him, like Judas kissing the Lord? Or do gestures like these really belong to the category of those tapping signs which prisoners use to transmit by code their walled-in loneliness from cell to cell? In order to be really near, don't we have to die, and start to live "far away"? Isn't it necessary for us first to have descended through death down into the heart of the world, in order to be near everything, near because in death we begin to live at the secret root of all things? Is not the body of flesh which we now carry around with us the limitation to a narrow here and now in this finite space and time, so that the only man who can be really close to all things is the man who by dying strips off this mortal flesh in order to put on the heavenly body?

"But he seems to be far away from me, and indeed, he himself said that he would leave us." No, not really; he was speaking only of relinquishing that earthly nearness, which, ultimately, is really distance. He was telling us that he would give no more tapping signs, that he would not need to, because he is no longer close-by in the dungeon of his passible, unglorified body. But now, through death and glorification, he is right in our midst, right here where we are, and not beside us, not merely next to us. "Behold, I am with you all days"!

And when he tells us through the Apostle that he is with us in his Spirit, through which he lives in us and we in him, when he lets us "put on" himself, he does not mean his holy commandments, nor his dispositions and attitudes, nor his theories and the prospects which he opens to us, but rather his actual spirit, the Spirit that proceeds from him as the living, given reality of his divine life. This is the life that streamed forth from his heart pierced in death, the life that penetrated into the innermost core of the world and the innermost core of our hearts. Because he wanted to come close to us definitively, he has gone away and has taken us with him. Because he was lifted up (on the cross of death and to the right hand of the Father), he and everything in him have become near. The reason for this is that his Spirit— the Spirit in whom Christ is near to us, the Spirit upon whom Christ from eternity to eternity bestows the eternal fullness of life from the Father, the Spirit over and above which there is nothing that Christ could give in all eternity—this Spirit is already in us now. He is in us as the basis of the nearness of eternal contemplation, as the basis of the transfiguration of the flesh. We notice nothing of this, and that is why the ascension seems to be separation. But it is separation only for our paltry consciousness. We must will to believe in such a nearness—in the Holy Spirit.

The ascension is the universal event of salvation history that must recur in each individual, in our personal salvation history through grace. When we become poor, then we become rich. When the lights of the world grow dark, then we are bathed in light. When we are apparently estranged from the nearness of his earthly flesh, then we are the more united with him. When we think we feel only a waste and emptiness of the heart, when all the joy of celebrating appears to be only official fuss, because the real truth around us cannot yet be admitted, then we are in truth better prepared for the feast of the Ascension than we might suppose. He takes on our semblance only to give us his own reality—the eternal, inexpressible reality that he received from the Father, that he gives us in his Spirit, and that we can receive because he, returning home with all that is ours, made it possible for us to share in God's own life.

XII

PENTECOST

PENTECOST COMPLETES Easter, for Pentecost is the completion of the saving events celebrated during Paschaltide. We
celebrated these events by recalling the sacrificial death of
the Lord, his victorious resurrection, and his entrance—by
means of his ascension—into his Father's eternity. All these
events took place so that the Holy Spirit might become our
portion. All these events have but one goal: to redeem the
world and the men in it, and to give God himself to this
redeemed world. That is why Pentecost is the fulfillment of
Easter. The reason why the glowing Love of the Father and
of the Son has descended into our hearts is that the Father's
own Son has brought our humanity back into the Father's
light. The reason why man can live God's own life in the
Holy Spirit is that the Son of Man died according to the flesh.
The Holy Spirit of the eternal God has come. He is here:
he lives in us, he sanctifies us, he strengthens us, he consoles
us. He is the pledge of eternal life, the earnest of absolute
triumph.

The center of all reality, the innermost heart of all infinity,
the love of the all-holy God has become our center, our heart.
True and absolute reality now lives in our nothingness; the
strength of God vitalizes our weakness: eternal life lives in
mortal man. The only thing that nightfall really means now
is that man cannot grasp the meaning of the day that has
dawned on him since Pentecost—the day that will see no

sunset. The tears of our despair and of our ever-recurring disappointments are nothing but trivial illusions that veil an eternal joy.

God is ours. He has not given us merely a gift, a gift created and finite like ourselves. No, he has given us his whole being without reserve: he has given us the clarity of his knowledge, the freedom of his love, and the bliss of his trinitarian life. He has given us himself. And his name is Holy Spirit. He is ours. He is in each heart that calls to him in humble faith. He is ours to such an extent that, strictly speaking, we can no longer say what man is if we omit the fact that God himself is man's possession. God is *our* God: that is the glad tidings of Pentecost.

That is the good news of Pentecost, the glorious, radiant message, the tidings of strength and of light and of victory, the message that God loves us and has blessed us with himself. That is the message. But do we give ear to this message, and do we grasp it with faith? I do not mean to ask whether we doubt it intellectually or whether we admit its validity with slightly less than full consent. But rather, has the message penetrated our hearts? Is it really there—in the bloodstream—and not merely there as one of our maxims (we have so many!), which we readily cite while living by entirely different standards? Is the good news of Pentecost in our heart of hearts as the light and strength of our lives? Or is it merely stirring rhetoric, pious words for the feast day, when we can treat ourselves to such ideals, because on feast days we are virtuous and do not have to work?

Do we live by the message? And, not only that, do we talk about it? Is our heart submissive enough to welcome as sheer grace the gift which is God himself, the gift which we can receive only on our knees in mute trembling before such a merciful God? Or is our heart so proud and self-assured that we think it only proper that God should visit us with his own personal life? Is our heart so haughty that it presumes to take such a grace for granted? Or is it so timid and despairing, so weary and empty, that it can really be satisfied only by its own poverty and weakness, because these things can be experienced, while possession by God's Spirit must be grasped by faith? In short, do we believe in the message of Pentecost?

Do we not have to cry out with the man in the Gospel, "I believe, Lord, help my unbelief" (Mk 9:24)? We must keep on asking, together with those who heard Saint Peter's Pentecost sermon, "Brethren, what shall we do?" (Acts 2:37). What shall we do, so that the Holy Spirit will be our portion, so that he will remain with us always, and continue to increase in us? Peter gave the answer to this question, and his answer is still valid for us: "Repent and be baptized every one of you in the name of Jesus Christ for the forgiveness of your sins; and you will receive the gift of the Holy Spirit" (Acts 2:38). The order of these two requisites may be reversed for us who have already been baptized; the demand itself still remains the same: baptism and, every day, a new conversion.

We are baptized. This is the first thing that God has done for us, and this assures us that he has willed to give us his Holy Spirit. Like the wind, the Spirit of God blows where he will, and in his loving patience he roams, no doubt, through all the streets of the world, in order there to touch men. And, in the omnipotence of his grace, he may find many to touch. Yet this grace always strives to bring such men home to its kingdom, the Church, and to incorporate them into the mystical body of Christ, whose soul is that same Spirit. But when his action takes place tangibly, in time and space, when it occurs not merely in the depths of the heart, but also in sign on the body, in word and water, when baptism is bestowed, then we know that here God surely lays his hands on man (if man does not obstruct his action) and he says:

"You are mine." Here God stamps his indestructible seal in the heart of man. Here, in the very depths of our being, the Father plants his Holy Spirit, his sacred strength, his divine life.

And this has happened to us. We are baptized. God has touched us, not merely by ideas and theories, not merely in pious moods and feelings, but by his own personal, incarnate action, which he works in us in baptism through his ordained servant. This is our consolation and our conviction: that God has already freely and openly spoken to us and poured the Spirit of his life into our hearts from the first days of our life. This clear testimony on the part of God is more impressive than the ambiguous testimony of our own heart in its weariness, weakness, and bitter emptiness. God has spoken in baptism: "You are my son and the holy temple of my own Spirit."

Compared with the divine word, of what value then is our everyday experience, the practical experience that makes us appear to be poor, God-forsaken and Spirit-forsaken creatures? Our faith is in God rather than in ourselves. We are baptized. And the delightful Spirit of God's life is in the depth of our being where man himself, perhaps, with his smattering of psychology, has not reached. There in those depths the Spirit speaks to the eternal God and says: "Abba, Father." There he addresses us: "Child, truly beloved child of everlasting life." We are baptized.

But if our baptism is recorded on the first page of the book of our life, we are not released from the second demand made by Peter on Pentecost: Repent. We can quench the Spirit, we can cause him grief, we can hinder him from bringing the blessed fruit of eternal life into us. And that is why we must open ourselves again each day to this Spirit of the Lord, turn to him again each day, be converted to him again each day.

We so-called good christians may often have the agonizing

impression that the Spirit of God has forgotten us. In our own lives and in the life of the Church, that great dwelling and temple of the Holy Spirit, we may often think that we are too little aware of the Spirit of God and his free but powerful sway. We may feel that we detect in and around us much of the letter and little of the Spirit, many commands and little freedom, much of external work and little heartfelt love, much fear and trembling and little bold trust, much duty and little charisma, much timid fear before God and little joyous confidence in his goodness, much love for the world and little for eternity. In short, we may think we find in and around us too much of the spirit of the world and too little of the Spirit of the Father. While these impressions may frequently be valid, there is usually something false in them, too. Something false, I say, because the human eye cannot detect the Spirit in us and in the Church. And if we feel how little we are truly men of the Spirit, we are usually once again ensnared in a false idea of God's Spirit and of his work in the Church. And that is the reason why daily conversion and reflection are especially necessary.

Ostensibly we seek the clarity of a faith that never falters, but in reality we want only a freedom from doubt that waters down our faith and its decision. We think we are seeking the Spirit of faith; yet instead of the certainty of the Spirit, who dwells in the darkness of faith, we are seeking only the clarity of earthly truisms.

Ostensibly we seek the power of the Spirit who overcomes the world, while in reality we desire a decisive triumph for the kingdom of God on earth, a triumph that would spare us from being patient and constant, even to the end. We think we seek the Spirit of divine power, but we desire the glory of the world instead of the power of the Spirit, who through patient love courts the hearts of men and their freely-returned love—even to the end.

Ostensibly we seek the freedom of the children of God in the Spirit of freedom; but in reality we really desire free rein for our laziness and our earthly tendencies. We think we are seeking the Holy Spirit of freedom, whereas we are seeking only the non-Spirit which binds a man in the fetters of his own selfishness, isolating him from other people, instead of drawing him into the freedom of the Spirit by first ushering him into the selfless love of God.

Ostensibly we seek the Spirit of holy joy, when in reality we desire leisurely entertainment that saves us from sharing in the tears of Christ and from shedding tears of repentance.

Ostensibly we seek the Spirit who gives life; yet in reality we desire only the non-Spirit who lies to us about life to lure us past the life that is gained only through death, to lure us where there is nothing but death.

We must reflect on all this, over and over again, every day. We must not interpret our experience of life falsely, and think that the Spirit of God has become distant and weak. Rather, we must learn from these experiences that we are always seeking him in the wrong place and in the wrong way, that we are always ready to confuse him with something else. If we reflect in this way, then we shall perceive over and over again with trembling joy that he is there, that he is with us: the Spirit of faith in darkness, the Spirit of freedom in obedience, the Spirit of joy in tears, the Spirit of eternal life in the midst of death. Then we are filled, in all the insignificance and silence of this world, in all the sober realism of everyday life, with the holy conviction that he is there, he is with us. He prays with unspeakable groanings in each one's heart. He consoles and strengthens, he heals and helps, he gives the certainty of eternal life. But we must reflect anew, each day.

Daily conversion enjoins yet a second activity: to pray for the Holy Spirit. The Church was in prayer when the Holy

Spirit came on Pentecost. He is the Spirit of grace—of grace that cannot be merited. He is the unfathomable marvel of God's love. Our deeds do not force him down from heaven, nor can the despairing cry of our distress compel him. He is and he remains, always and in each moment, the free gift from above. In the very moment when we decide to seize upon him as something which belongs to us by right, he will withdraw. On the other hand, when we wait, expecting nothing from ourselves, when we reckon with the incalculable, when we call to one who has no name, when we are confident without referring to anything that is in ourselves, then we pray, we pray for the Holy Spirit. And then the Holy Spirit comes, gently perhaps, and unnoticeably, but really. He comes not because we pray, but because God wills to love us. Then the Holy Spirit comes, because the Spirit of God himself, praying in us, has called out to himself. If we realize that we are unprofitable servants—how hard this is, and yet so obvious—then the reward of unprofitable servants, the Holy Spirit, is already there. If we confess our weakness— how hard this is and yet so obvious—then we are praying, and then the strength of our weakness, the Holy Spirit, is already with us.

Everything that we are, therefore, prays in us for the Holy Spirit of the Father and of the Son. The recognition that we are outcasts before God, our weakness—even our sinfulness, which causes us to lose God's word through carelessness, our poverty, weakness and darkness, even our coldness towards God and his holy love—everything that is in us prays in mute expectancy for the Holy Spirit of the Father and of the Son.

Come, Spirit, Spirit of the Father and of the Son. Come, Spirit of love, Spirit of sonship, Spirit of peace, of faith, of strength, of holy joy. Come, secret joy, into the tears of the world. Come, victory-rich life, into the death of the earth.

Come, Father of the poor, support of the oppressed. Come, Love, who is poured out into our hearts. We have nothing that can force you; yet on that very account we are confident. Our hearts stand in mysterious awe at your coming, because you are selfless and gentle, because you are something else than our heart. Yet this is for us the firmest promise that you are nevertheless coming. Come, therefore, come to us every day, again and again. We put our trust in you. Where else could we trust? We love you because you are love itself. In you we have God for our Father, because you cry out in us, "Abba, Father." We thank you, quickening Spirit, Holy Spirit, we thank you for dwelling in us, for having willed to be in us the seal of the living God, the seal that stamps us as his property. Do not forsake us in the bitter struggle that is life; do not forsake us at the end when everything else will abandon us. *Veni, Sancte Spiritus.*

XIII

CORPUS CHRISTI

THE PROCESSION is both the most external element connected with the feast of Corpus Christi, and it is also its distinguishing factor. When, however, what is external springs entirely from within, as it does here, then the external is also the revelation of the inner kernel. And that is why it is possible to contemplate the mystery of this feast from the point of view of the procession.

The Corpus Christi procession originated in the last part of the thirteenth century. At the beginning of the fifteenth century, it had already become a universal custom. It is a relic of the late Middle Ages and of their unity of faith, and so it is not a demonstration of faith against a non-Catholic world. It originated from the general custom of having field-processions. The people who marched in these processions brought with them the tools of their everyday life. They carried the "holy ones" (the relics belonging to the Church, even to the "most holy One") into every aspect of their life.

Because even in their diversity all these people sprang from one root and aspired to one end, in the procession they intertwined the spheres and activities of their lives. The wide open spaces became their Church, the sun became the candles for the altar, the fresh breeze joined with the songs of the people to make one choir, the altars stood at the intersection of everyday life. The solemn gathering of people standing before God became a colorful, happy procession of marchers, and the carefree birds of the air winged their flight through the prayers that rose from the troubled earth—prayers that already were almost transformed into pure song of praise. Thus the procession is both the visible expression of man's movement through the space of his existence towards his goal, and the shining forth of the holy One, who is himself the support of this procession, who steadfastly stays with it, and who leads it to its proper goal, who is God.

From this point of view, we come to the significance of the feast of Corpus Christi: to the significance of the Eucharist. Certainly this sacrament reaches its full significance when it is received. Even when we keep it on our altars and when we carry it through the regions where we live, uplifted and in full sight, still it is always the food which we wholly make our own only when we eat it. Yet this sacrament is an enduring sacrament that can and should be preserved, shown, and worshipped, just as in daily life we are ready to eat the food that we long for and that our eye sees. And so the essence of the sacrament of the altar also shows forth when it is seen and honored as the sacrament that endures, even if what it contains does not appear so clearly as it does when we receive the sacrament in sign and reality.

Seen in this way, what is the first thing that the Corpus Christi procession tells us? It tells us—or rather through it we remind ourselves—that we are pilgrims on the earth. We have here no lasting dwelling place. We are a people who change, who are restlessly driven on through time and space, who are *in via*, and still seeking our real homeland and our everlasting rest. We are those who must allow themselves to be changed, because to be a member of the human race means to let oneself change, and perfection means to have changed often. The movement of the procession makes perfectly clear our dependence on time and the stratification of the sphere of our existence.

But this procession is not merely a throng, and its motion is not only the mass flight of those who are hurrying through time and the barren desert of earthly existence. A procession is a holy movement of those truly united. It is a gentle stream of peaceful majesty, not a procession of fists clenched in bitterness, but of hands folded in gentleness. It is a procession which threatens no one, excludes no one, and whose blessing even falls on those who stand astonished at its edge and who look on, comprehending nothing. It is a movement which the holy One, the eternal One supports with his presence; he gives peace to the movement and he gives unity to those taking part in it. The Lord of history and of this holy exodus from exile towards the eternal homeland himself accompanies the exodus. It is a holy procession, one that has a goal, both before it and with it. From this point of view, we can understand the specific significance of this procession.

It tells us of the eternal presence of human guilt in the history of mankind and in our own history; yes, even in the history of my life. With us on our march we carry the Body which was given for us. The cross of Calvary goes with us, the sign that the guilt of deicide weighs upon mankind. The body and the life that we all have crushed in death goes with us. This procession of sinners tells us that in our journey through time we always have the crucified One with us. When we walk down our streets, past houses where dwell sinful luxury, sinful misery and darkness of hearts, then we are walking past new manifestations of this sin of the world. When we walk right into the midst of these manifestations, then we are proclaiming his death, which we are all guilty of, and our death. Through this procession, which is accompanied by the crucified One, we acknowledge that we are sinners and that we have to suffer our own guilt and that of all mankind. We confess that again and again we walk down the path of error, of guilt, and of death, the path which the sinless One also walked for us and always continues to walk with us—in the sacrament and in the grace of his Spirit. This path has mysteriously become redemption for those who believe with love, who understand this sacrament, and who take it with them on their dark path.

The procession tells us of the abiding presence of Christ, our reconciliation on the paths of our life. He goes with us, he who is reconciliation, he who is love and mercy. During all the time that we call life, as we trudge along the streets of this earth, he is there, right behind us, pursuing us in the obstinacy of his love. He follows us, even when we walk down a crooked path and lose our direction. He seeks the lost sheep even in the wilderness, and he runs to meet the prodigal son. He walks with us on the pilgrimage of our life, he who walked down all these streets himself—*quaerens me sedisti lassus*—from birth to death. He therefore knows how we feel on this endless journey that is so often trackless. He is near at hand, visible and invisible, with the mercy of his heart, with the patient and full and merciful experience of his whole human life. He, salvation itself, and the propitiation of our sins. We carry the sacrament through the fields and wilderness of our life, and give testimony that as long as he goes with us we have with us the one who can make every way straight and purposeful.

The procession tells us of a blessed wonder: since the incarnation and death and resurrection of Christ, our movement in the procession is not only towards a goal, but we already move right in the midst of the goal itself. Indeed, the end of the ages has already come over us. Yes, we wandering pilgrims already carry in our hands the one who is himself our end and our goal. We lift up the body in which divinity and humanity are already indissolubly united. We carry the glorified body (although still hidden under the veils of this world) in which the world, in a moment that belongs to her forever, has already begun to be glorified and to tower up into the eternal, inaccessible light of God himself. The motion of the world, so the Corpus Christi procession tells us, has already entered upon its last phase, and as a whole it can no longer miss its goal. The distant goal of this motion of all millenia has already mysteriously penetrated into the movement itself. It is there not merely as promise and as a far distant future, but as reality and presence.

We sing, *Et antiquum documentum novo cedat ritui;* we should also grasp all that this means. Gone is the alliance of promise, of experiment and of provision; gone is the history that is still open and still experimentally seeking its goal by trial and error. The eternal and definitive One, God himself, is already there. There is a mysterious moment when time and eternity, earth and heaven, God and man—two poles, separated by an eternity, yet coming up to meet one another —even begin to penetrate each other. In this moment and in this place, the procession that carries the body of the Lord takes place; it is the expression of this moment and of this point.

Novum Pascha novae legis Phase vetus terminat. Through the new covenant, the new Paschal Lamb brought the old alliance to an end. This procession carries the already glorified body of him who forever is inseparably God and man, and thus it tells us that our motion has already— mysteriously, yet really—taken into itself its definitive goal. This procession also tells us about the unity that exists between the persons walking in the procession. Mankind moves through all the vast spheres of its histories, its cultures, its states and wars, its summits and abysses. Yet this motion is more than men running helter-skelter in confusion and chaos, more than the chaotic haste of those who, throughout their whole life, are pursued by the bare necessities of life, by utopian ideals and by diabolical powers. They already have unity bestowed upon them, freely and graciously, both among themselves and in their motion. According to Saint Paul, we are all one body, we who eat of the one bread. Sign of unity and bond of love, is what Augustine calls the body which the pilgrims of history in loving faith carry into the market place of their lives in this holy procession. They lift it in blessing over the earth—the earth from which they can scarcely earn their bread. They lift it over the earth which greedily drinks their blood and their tears, so that eventually (but only provisionally) the body will have to pass away into the seemingly aimless history of nature.

We carry the body of the Lord in holy procession and by this action we proclaim that we are one, that we are walking the same path, the one path of God and his eternity. The same power of eternal life is already working in all of us: the one divine love is already our portion. Our share in this love binds us together more deeply and more inwardly than anything that could unite or even separate us in the past. The sacrament of the unity of the Church and of all the redeemed—this is what we carry throughout life. We thus give witness to the love that moves the sun and the other stars, to the love that is impelling both humanity and the entire cosmos towards that goal and into that one kingdom in which God will be all in all.

We are pilgrims and aliens who have here no lasting dwelling place. We are still seeking what is to come and what is to abide forever: the supreme goal and the everlasting rest which is, quite simply, life itself. But we are pilgrims whose success is accompanied by the mercy of God, pilgrims who already have their goal in their possession, since what we already have and already are has only to be made manifest. We are pilgrims of an unending motion towards the goal and in the goal, pilgrims of a single goal, who are one in love through the one bread of eternal life.

Let us walk indefatigably, today and forever, on all the streets of this life, the smooth and the rough, the blissful and the bloodied. The Lord is nearby; the goal and the strength of the way is there. Under God's heaven a holy procession moves on the streets of the earth. It will arrive at its goal. For already—this day, in fact—heaven and earth join together and celebrate one blessed feast.

XIV

SACRED HEART

"CRIMSON MYSTERY OF ALL THINGS"—the Church speaks in a hymn by Gertrude von le Fort—"solitary Heart, all-knowing Heart, world-conquering Heart." According to the metaphysical dialogues of Hedwig Conrad-Martius, the heart is "the center of man. His whole being, as it gives birth to itself in soul, body and mind, unfolds and gushes forth. It is again taken up into and established in this one center. Here, as it were, it is tied together and fastened centrally; the whole 'bloodstream,' every path of personal life, runs together into it, in order to go out again from it. Man can say, will, and do nothing as a total person that does not spring from this center in which alone his whole being is established in unity. In a personal sense, all else is empty, unsubstantial, and unreal."

The "heart" is the name we give to the unifying element in man's diversity. The heart is that ultimate ground of a man's being. His diversity of character, thought and activity springs from this ground. All that he is and does unfolds from this source. His diversity, originally one in its source, remains one even in its unfolding, and it ultimately returns to this unity.

The "heart" is the name we give to the inner ground of a man's character, wherein a man is really himself, unique and alone. Man's apartness, his individuality, his interiority, his solitariness—this is what we call the heart. This characteristic of the heart reveals and at the same time veils itself in everything that man is and does. For man's total diversity in being and activity would be nothing if it did not blossom forth from man's heart as from a living ground, and at the same time veil this hidden ground. It must be veiled because its water doesn't flow on the surface of what we commonly speak of as man's being and activity.

A man's uniqueness, his individuality, is his heart. That is why man is always alone and solitary—alone and solitary in the meaning that everyday life gives to the words, in the idiom of the market-place, which no longer suspects the abysses concealed in human words. For there is a realm where man is entirely himself, where he himself is his solitary destiny. In this realm where he can no longer bring himself and his fragmentized world to the market of everyday life— in the realm, therefore, where his heart is—man is alone and solitary because of this apartness of his being and his activity. He is alone because the heart is never a generic concept, never a coin that can find its way through many hands; because the heart belongs always—yes, only—to itself and to the God who created it.

And that is the reason why only the *heart* knows in the full sense of the word. For man properly knows only what is proper to him. Whatever else he knows, he knows only because it is this sphere of his own being, the world, into which he pours out the diversity of his life, or because it is the mystery of his unique heart, the mystery that is God. That is why really interior knowledge, knowledge that really grasps something completely and is more than a list of indifferent facts, is knowledge of the heart, man's center, which knows by experience and by suffering—his center, where spirit and body, light and love dwell together undivided in one chasm. The heart is all-knowing in its apartness because all that it knows it knows in *one*, because it is in possession of itself.

But what is this solitary, all-knowing heart of man in which the world is perceived and concentrated, the heart that is the ground of man and of all his activity? Is this being perishable or is it substantial? Shadow or reality? Death or life? Is Scripture's final word on the heart (it is mentioned in about a thousand places) the bitter wisdom of Ecclesiastes (7:4): *Cor sapientium, ubi tristitia est, et cor stultorum, ubi laetitia* ("The heart of the wise tarries in the house of sadness, and the heart of the fool in the house of mirth"); *or* is it the faith of Peter (2 Pet 1:19) that the morningstar rises in the heart and that peace exults eternally?

When a person collects himself in his heart, when all being and doing finally flow back from dispersion into that one ground that we call the heart, what happens there? What does man experience when in his heart he experiences what he possesses as his own, what he really is? Is this ground nothingness or fullness? Is there fullness and reality only in diversity, and is apartness only a pitiful loneliness? Does the solitary heart border on infinity, or is it, as the end of all things and all reality, the place where apartness comes to itself in order to trickle away into its own finiteness and come to despair? Does heart mean the mouth of all the brooks of our being, the mouth that leads into eternity, or is it the gate through which all dying reality is pressed down, weak and tired, to everlasting death? Is the flowing together of all our diverse activities into the heart the end of the delusion that we might be something, because diversity that is not gathered up causes us to fail to notice that all this diversity really adds up to zero?

Doesn't it seem that a person can appear all the more constricted and empty—even in the experience of daily life— the more collected he is; and all the richer, the more dispersed and diffused he is? Doesn't it seem that whoever possesses himself has just himself alone, and only he who loses himself can possess another? Is not gathering to the one heart in this manner the dispersion of everything, and is not dispersion into everything the only gathering possible to it? Is there, then, no apartness, and is the only apartness that exists the apartness of an empty heart?

This, then, is the ultimate need, the innermost misery, the misery of the heart: that the heart of man (the ultimate center of the world) only seems to be the place where man's own poverty is frightened concerning itself, and the place where, at best, the finitude of all things—which could never be all in one—is unmasked. Do we have to *love* and *seek* our heart, because only in this way are we in possession of our-selves? Or do we have to hate and flee, because we possess in our ground, the heart, only the nothingness of our own being?

Of course, we are ready with a quick answer. So quick that it would perhaps be better if we did not have it at hand *so* quickly that as a result we no longer understand the question. We answer: "God." Yes, this is the answer, the whole answer, supposing only that we understand it. Indeed, he is the apartness, who is fullness and not emptiness, who is life and not death. He is the central point, the heart of the world, in whom all reality is gathered up and yet is not pressed together in a stifling corner. He is the unfathomable womb, in which everything shines brightly, however. He is the unity which is not purchased at the price of denial. Down from his mountains all waters eternally gush in a torrent, and the chambers of these mountains stay just as eternally full. He is not, as we are, merely the heart of one solitary person, but the heart of all reality, the all-in-one inwardness of all things. He exists before all multiplicity and dispersion, and he never needs such multiplicity, to be everything. He can be of one mind without being unilateral; he can be all without being all-common.

But have we found an answer for the distress, the misery, the need of our heart? If we say that "God" is the answer, have we really named the heart of our hearts? Does that answer of itself tell us that the apartness of *our* heart, too, is fullness and not emptiness, reality and not despairing loneliness? Does that answer tell us that the inner awareness of our all-knowing heart embraces the infinite and not our nothingness? Doesn't our heart, the center of our being, run into extreme danger precisely through this answer, given so quickly? For if he is the heart of our hearts—even though as philosophers we quickly and confidently say that he is—is the need of our hearts then banished, or have we just named its ultimate need?

So easily do we explain God as the heart of our hearts with worldly wisdom, and fancy that by saying this we have said that the full oneness and the one fullness is ours, the fullness that fills our empty oneness, without its having to go out in complete dispersion.

But even if we say that God is the mystery of our hearts, the salvation of our heart's need, then, if we reflect rightly, it may appear to us in fear and trembling that it is most frightful to have God as the center of our center. For is not his own infinity, in which everything is the same, bearable only for him? *He*, of course, is always everything in each of his attributes and in each of his works. He has his *whole* heart in all that he is and in all that he does, so that with him everything is always fruitful and *at the same time* inward. But what if he comes to us in this way? Then he would be "all in each" for *us* too. When he enters into our life he does not need to be particularly concerned that the lightning flash of his omnipotence should also be for him the soft light of his wisdom. He can let his *whole* being roar into our life in its power, and yet his waters have flowed from nowhere at all and have released no possibility that he does not fill with his reality. He can overpower us as inexorable justice, and to his ear the eternal judgment to damnation is still the jubilation that praises his boundless goodness.

But for us and for our narrowness it is precisely this that is frightful and terrifying, it is just this that causes all the seams of our finiteness to sag apart. He is always his whole self. He is always his heart, in whatever way he may treat us—whether he loves us or passes us by, whether his power or his goodness is revealed to us, whether his justice or his mercy comes over us.

But precisely because he thus is and remains the *one*, the all-one infinity of all being (however he may manifest himself to us), when we appeal to his all-one infinity, *we* do not know how he will act towards us. When we boldly declare that he is the heart of our heart, we do not know whether justice or grace will become the center of our hearts. Just when we want to use his heart so that the needed calculation of our heart will come out right, we write the enigmatic number of his ambiguous infinity and the figuring of our heart becomes all the more a really insoluble riddle. How insane it would be to ponder over him and count up his attributes, if we could not know whether they fall on us as an annihilating flash of lightning or as a dew that brings blessing. All the wisdom of the world cannot know this. For it has never known about God's judgment, under which we have all fallen. But without this all truth remains either tragic naiveté or malice.

The center of our hearts has to be God; the heart of the world has to be the heart of our hearts. He must send us his heart so that our hearts may be at rest. It has to be *his* heart. But it must not be the heart that embraces each and every thing in unfathomable unity. He must make as the center of our being a heart that is really the heart of the infinite God, and that *nonetheless* is a heart that is not everything, a heart that does not signify only *one*, a heart that is not only the ground of *one*. For the mortal fear over his ambiguous infinity and for the need of our hearts to depart from us, he has to let his heart become finite. He must let it become the unequivocality that is our life. He must let it enter into our narrow confines, so that it can be the center of our life without destroying the narrow house of our finitude, in which alone we can live and breathe.

And he has done it. And the name of his heart is: Jesus Christ! It is a finite heart, and yet it is the heart of God. When it loves us and thus becomes the center of our hearts, every need, every distress, every misery of our hearts is taken from us. For his heart is God's heart, and yet it does not have the terrifying ambiguity of his infinity. Up from this heart and out from this heart human words have arisen, intimate words, words of the heart, words of God that have only *one* meaning, a meaning that gladdens and blesses.

Our heart becomes calm and rests in this heart, in his heart. When it loves us, then we know that the love of such a heart is only love and nothing else. In him the enigmatic mystery of the world's heart which is God becomes the crimson mystery of all things, the mystery that God has loved the world in its destitution.

Only in this heart do we know who God wills to be for us. Only by it, the heart of Christ, is the riddle, into which all the wisdom of the world leads us, changed into the mystery of love that gladdens and blesses. In the heart of Christ our heart is all-knowing because it knows the one fact without which all knowledge is vanity and spiritual nuisance and without which all the practical experience of our heart causes only despair: in the heart of Christ our heart knows that it is one with *the* heart of God. It knows that it is one with the heart of God in which even the thief and the murderer find pardon, one with the heart in which our deepest, darkest nights are transformed into days, because he has endured the nights with us. It knows that it is one with the heart in which everything is transformed into the one love.

If he is our heart, our diversity can enter into the apartness of God without being burned to nothing in it. In him our dispersion can be collected without being confined and constricted, our heart can gush forth into the expanse of the world without being lost. The heart of Jesus is God's heart in the world, in which alone the world finds its God as its blessed mystery, in which alone God becomes the heart of our hearts, in which our being finds its center: at one and the same time unified and all-embracing.

XV

THE ASSUMPTION

TODAY WE celebrate the feast of Mary's Assumption. After her quiet death, the Blessed Virgin and Mother of God entered, body and soul, into eternal life, the life of God himself. In Mary's case, too, the fruit of death was life, and so this feast is also the anniversary day of a death. It is a question of that mysterious moment when time and eternity, transitoriness and immortality touch one another in the existence of one human being, the moment when a mortal man enters the house of his eternity. From this point of view we shall attempt to come a little closer to the mystery of this feast.

If we examine the life of man as it appears to us externally and immediately, we find in him—as in all things—that common trait of being bound up with and limited by time. Everything breathes the breath of evanescence, every earthly thing lives only a moment, laboriously joining one tiny interval to the next, just as one breath follows the other, so that life may continue. And each period of time, each breath, can be the last. Each is born only for a little while, first one, and only then the next. As we seize the next, the first escapes from us, and no power calls it back to life again. So, everything that we do—whether in the inner life of the soul or in the external work of the body—takes place in this temporal order. Everything is endlessly a coming and a going. Men come into existence and pass away; they are born and they die. Everything that has its beginning here on earth must someday come to an end. The shout of joy will someday fade away; all misery will one day be wept out; someday all power will vanish like smoke. Vanity of vanities, moaned Coheleth.

How strangely vain and puny, in a certain sense, must all our activity be: no matter how great it may have been, it cannot endure, but passes away. It hastens away as soon as possible to hide its insignificance in the empty darkness of the past. This is probably why men, whose hands tremble with greed and with secret horror in the face of death, snatch up in this short interval, in this short dream that we call life, as much pleasure and honor, power and knowledge as they can. But the vessel is narrow, and everything that we pour into it is finite. Both the wine of joy and the bitter water of suffering are always coming to nothing. Everything ends in death.

The immortal soul seems to be only the ground over which marches the ghastly procession of things and actions destined for death. The soul seems to exist only for this purpose, that the eternal succession of all thoughts, actions, and feelings that flutter past may be eternally accompanied by the painful knowledge of their transitory nature. The soul seems to exist only for the purpose of whispering to each moment of success the bitter truth that it shall pass away like the success that was previously experienced and seen to pass away. All living is dying.

Still there is something in these things that does not pass away. Every wave of time that seems to rise only to sink back as if it had never existed lifts something up that it does not take back again into the frightening emptiness of the past. In the indifference of all coming and going there mysteriously lives something full of meaning, something eternal: good and evil. It is as if every wave of time in its restless rise and fall is continually beating against the shore of eternity, and each wave, each moment of time, each human deed leaves there what is eternal in it: the good and the evil. Good and evil are things of eternity; they are eternity in the things of time.

It is at once a comforting and a frightful mystery: our deeds sink into nothingness, but before they die they give birth to an eternal property that does not disappear with them. The eternal goodness and badness of our perishable works sink down into the eternal "ground" of our imperishable soul, and shape this hidden ground. Even if new transitory waters keep rushing over this deep ground of the soul, neither time nor forgetting obliterates what goodness and badness have brought about in those depths. Only new goodness and repentance can make good what evil has done there for eternity; and only new evil can still destroy the hidden beauty of the goodness there. Only evil, not time; not what is transitory.

In this way the eternal countenance of our soul—and in it our eternal destiny—slowly develops while we exist in this transitory state. And then the moment comes when a man passes out of the temporal order into eternity. When this happens, a stream of transitoriness vanishes forever. The restless fluctuation of time ceases to surge over a soul in endless rise and fall, and it sets free the ground of the soul that until now was seen by God alone. The eternal countenance of the soul is now revealed—the countenance that was hidden in the depths, veiled by the haze of this life on earth. What exists now, what has endured, is eternal; and we are eternal because of what we have thus become in time. This means that a man travels the path of his life through time into an eternity that is no longer time.

Mary has traveled this path. Today we celebrate the day when for her time became eternity. She too led this life of transitoriness. With her as with all the children of this earth, life was a restless coming to be and passing away. Her life began quietly and obscurely, somewhere in a corner of Palestine, and soon it was snuffed out, gently, and the world knew it not. In between these two points, her life was filled with the same restless change that constitutes our life, and it was filled with the cares common to all Eve's children: anxiety for bread, suffering and tears, and a few small joys. So too were her hours measured out to her: a few hours of the utmost happiness in God her Savior joined with many routine, ordinary hours of grief, one after another, lusterless, feeble, and seemingly so empty and dull. But finally all the hours, the sublime as well as the ordinary, had passed away; and they could all now appear as one insignificant whole, precisely because they could thus fade away into the past.

Mary's life was a life of transitoriness, just like our own. And yet, in one respect it was entirely different. How enigmatic and incomprehensible our life is, not because of the darkness of fate—Mary, too, had her share in this common loss—but because of guilt. This is what makes our life so paradoxical and so confused. In our life, the eternal that makes up a part of our moments is sometimes good, sometimes evil. And when through God's grace a moment of repentance blots out what the evil hours would have made eternal in the depths of our being, even then there is one effect still left: these evil hours are gone forever; they are forever empty. Never again will a bright eternity issue from their womb, for they have sunk back fruitless into the nothingness of hours that "have been." No man can fetch them back again to relive them in the present, to make them good. Never again will the radiant light of the goodness that shall shine like an everlasting dawn rest upon them.

We know of only one person besides Jesus who can enter into eternity without repentance. This is Mary, the ever-pure

Virgin, the immaculate one. What our heart in its bitter experience can hardly believe has become true for one human being—Mary. She need not disclaim one moment of her life; no part of it has remained empty and dead. She can stand by each deed of her life: not one was dark; not one passed away without enkindling an eternal light, without shining with the luminosity that entirely consumes the moral possibilities of each moment. Such a life did not come to an end with Mary's death; when she died, only the transitory died, so that what was eternal in her life might be revealed—that eternal light from the many thousand candles enkindled by each moment of her life. Thus, her whole life entered eternity—each day, each hour, each breaking of the waves of the life of her soul, every joy and every pain, the great and the small hours. Nothing was abandoned; everything lives on in the eternal goodness of the soul that has gone home.

Is not such a day a day of joy for us? We know, indeed, from our own experience, that our constantly changing human life hurries on towards its eternity, to its everlasting destiny. But when the last moment of time that is meted out to a man has come, then his mouth is closed in death, and his eyes no longer transmit a glimpse of his soul; only an enigmatic death mask looks at us—and he is silent. It is as if the passageway of death had two gates, and when man steps into this passageway, he closes the first gate behind him before he opens the second, so that no light shines through to us from that land that lies beyond the passageway. Is it not wonderfully consoling, then, that our faith tells us of that world into which the dead have gone and of their eternal destiny? What can move us most deeply in all this is that this witness of faith does not merely give us information about the objective, impersonal possibilities that can begin after death. It is rather as if God's revelation, which speaks to us of the life of God hidden in inaccessible light, reveals to us more than that life's blessedness. The very same word of God speaks also of the holy lives of those who rest eternally in the merciful heart of God. God affectionately calls each one by name: Peter, with his repentance and three-fold love, is with me; Paul, the great warrior and long-sufferer is, with me; Francis, the happy beggar, is with me; Benedict Labre is with me, and he spent his life begging on the highway; Stanislaus is with me, and he was simply a pious, brave child. And so God still has many names for us: he has called us by countless names. He has thereby willed to entrust to us a sweet mystery of his heart; he has, as it were, placed us in intimate contact with those whom he has sheltered forever in his heart as his child, his friend, his betrothed. And thus we know that a blessed soul's quite fixed life—a life which cannot be repeated once it is lived, which we can call by name, which we can narrate, in the paths of which we follow, which we love and honor and which calls us to imitation— this life has not disappeared, but still lives. With meaning and profit let each moment of such a life pass before us once again and we can say again and again: the goodness that inspired that fixed deed still shines unimpaired and bright in the soul; the heroic spirit that sacrificed its life at that instant has outlived death.

That is why the Church celebrates feast upon feast of her saints, fresh again every day, birthdays of an eternity, victory-feasts of imperishable goodness, feasts of delight because love never ceases. They rouse us anew every day from tired resignation to transitoriness: it is not true that everything passes away, for the good is immortal. Wherever in this world only a tiny light of purity, of kindness, of humility, of fortitude, of patience shines, it burns on before God's eternal light as the reflection of his own eternally blessed light. And just as the mysterious God is quite close to us in faith because his own reality brings the shining rays of his beauty to the eye of our faith, so too, in the same faith, these holy men of eternity are close to us; the beauty of their goodness completes our love. It is as if each one gently touches our soul, and we can say to each in words of love: I am joyful over your eternal goodness, you are very close to me, and your goodness is an eternal victory.

Thus it is with the Virgin Mary. In faith we know that the charming splendor of grace that already filled her soul when the word of her Maker called her into being is still an indestructible reality. The tender humility, the brightness of her grand spirit, the boundless submission to God—everything that filled her soul when she said, "I am the handmaid of the Lord"—all this is always present and new. The simple greatness of her life, the sacrifice of her Son under the cross: all this goodness and holiness that once brightened this dark world is eternal life that now, at this very hour, mixes its roar with the waves of divine life in the eternal today.

As eternal life slowly came into being during her earthly existence, all that was once broken up and then vanished into the past has streamed together into a superabundance of bliss in the one now of eternity. This now of eternity, always the same and always new, beyond all time, sees how in the uttermost depths time makes its way.

And only the thin veil of this earthly life lies between us and this perpetual rejoicing—a veil through which the light of faith and the voice of God, who is a God of the living, penetrate. And these give witness of the eternal life of the most pure Virgin. For him who in yearning and longing reaches out for it, isn't her gracious heart close to us through the nearness of faith and of love, through the still, holy nearness of eternity?

When we, from the depths of our dying day, greet this eternal today, we will be greeted with the same endlessness of eternal life that has been roaring for two thousand years (in human measurement) and that shall never vanish. And then we reflect that this eternity rises up out of the dark valleys of our transitoriness, and we look up full of blessed hope, because in Mary's bliss we see prefigured the blessed destiny that our soul shall one day find. If it is true that we merit more love the purer and holier we are, then whose love are we indebted to, if not that of the most Blessed Virgin and mother of Jesus? When we love goodness, we should be enthused by the thought that Mary's incomprehensible goodness is now blessed and preserved in eternity.

Thus we are blessed in the pure, unselfish joy that the goodness, purity, and all the virtues that we love have achieved an eternal victory through the most Blessed Virgin. We sense that her victory is our own. We know, too, that the goodness that today has become eternity was not on that account taken away from us, but works among us in blessing and grace.

That is why we should fold our hands and pray: Holy Mary, Mother of God, pray for us sinners now in this transitoriness, which was also yours, and in the hour of our death, so that we may enter into the eternity that today is yours.

XVI

ALL SAINTS DAY

ALL SAINTS DAY and All Souls Day are the feasts of every
saint and of every soul who has died and gone home into the
eternal love of God. *All* of them and therefore not only those
already celebrated by name in the Church's feasts throughout
the year but also the silent, unknown ones who have departed
as if they had never even existed. There are no legends about
them; their lives are recorded neither in poetry nor in history,
secular or ecclesiastical. Only one person knows anything
about these saints, and that is God. He has inscribed their
names in the book of life, which is the heart of his eternal
love.

But we are supposed to celebrate these saints who are not
known to us by name. How can we do this—really do it, with
life and zest—if not by lovingly remembering our dead? They
may already be forgotten by the world; perhaps their name
is not even inscribed on a gravestone. Yet they not only live
on with God, but also with us, in our hearts.

Let us then prepare our hearts for these feasts of the dead
who live with God. May our hearts be mindful of the dead.
Be still, O heart, and let all whom you have loved rise from
the grave of your breast. Is there no one among All Saints
and All Souls for you to celebrate? Have you ever come in
contact with love and meekness, goodness and purity and
fidelity in a person? Not even in your mother, so quiet and
forgetful of herself? Nor in your patient father? Should you
say no, I think you would be contradicting your heart,

137

which has its own experiences. It is not the heart's experience to have met throughout life only darkness and no light, only selfishness and no selfless kindness.

But if you have met faith, hope and love, kindness and pardon, great courage and fidelity in persons who now are dead—a grain of virtue such as these is worth a mountain of selfishness and vice—then you have met men whom your heart may seek with God. Up, then, and celebrate the heart-feast of All Saints, of All Souls—*your* saints, *your* beloved souls! Sorrow and joy, grief and happiness are strangely blended into this feast. Just as they are with the things of eternity. Celebrate an All Saints of peace and loyalty. Of yearning and of faith. Celebrate your dead who are still living.

Today then, we want to remember before God our dead, all those who once belonged to us and who have departed from us. There are so many of them that we can by no means take them all in at one glance. If our celebration is to greet them all, we must go back in memory over our path through life. When we go about it in this way, from our point of view it is like a procession of persons marching down the street of life.

At each moment, without bidding farewell, someone or other silently withdraws from the procession and, turning aside from the road, is lost in the darkness of the night. This procession becomes smaller and smaller for each one of us, for the new men constantly stepping onto our path through life only seem to be marching along with us. To be sure, many are walking the same street, but only a few walk *together with* each one of us. Strictly speaking, only those who set out together with each one of us are really journeying together with us. Only those who were with us at the very beginning of our journey to God—only those who were and still are really close to our heart.

The others are travelling companions on the same road; they are many, and they are constantly coming and going. We greet each other, and give each other a helping hand, and then, no more. But the real procession of each of our lives is made up of those whom we really love. This procession is always becoming smaller and quieter, until each one of us becomes silent once and for all, turns aside from the road, and passes away without a farewell, never to return.

That is why our heart today is with those who have already departed in just such a way. There are no replacements for them; no other man could really fill the vacancy left by a loved one when he suddenly and unexpectedly departs and is at our side no longer. In true love no one can replace the beloved, for true love loves the beloved in those depths where each man is uniquely and irreplaceably himself. That is why each one of those who have passed away has taken a part of our heart with him: they may be said even to have taken the heart with them, if death has trodden through our lives from beginning to end.

If a man has really loved and continues to love, then even before his own death his life is changed into a life with the dead. Could the lover forget his dead? If one has really loved, then his forgetting and the fact that he has ceased weeping are not signs that nothing has really changed, that he is just the same as before. They are, rather, signs that a part of his own heart has really died with the loved one, and is now living with the dead. That is why he can no longer mourn. We live, then, with the dead, with those who have gone before us into the dark night of death, where no one can work any more.

But how are we supposed to be able to live with the dead in the one reality of our mutual love; how are we to celebrate a feast of all the holy dead? Is this possible simply because God is the God of the living and not of the dead, because his word and even the wisdom of this world tells us that these dead still live? Because we loved the dead and still love them, we must be with them always. But are they also with us? Do they belong to this love and to the celebration of this love?

They have departed, they are silent. No word from them reaches our ears; the gentle kindness of their love no longer fills our heart. How quiet the dead are, how *dead* they are! Do they want us to forget them, as we forget a casual acquaintance on a trip, with whom we exchanged a few insignificant words? If life is not taken away from those who depart this life in God's love, but changed into eternal, measureless, superabundant life, why then should it seem to us that they no longer exist? Is the inaccessible light of God into which they have entered so faint that it cannot penetrate to us down here? Does even their love (and not only their bodies) have to abandon us in order to live with God in his light? Does their silence imitate the silence of their God, to whose home they have gone?

That is the way it is. For God is silent just like the dead. For us to celebrate his feasts in our hearts, this silent God must certainly be with us, even though he seems so distant and so silent. We certainly must love him, too, as we love our dead, the distant and silent dead, who have entered into the night. Does he not give to our love an intelligible answer when we call him to the feast of the heart, and ask him for a sign that his love exists for us and is present to us? And that is why we cannot lament the silence of the dead, for their silence is only an echo of his silence.

But if we keep silent and meek, if we listen to this silence of God's, then we begin to grasp with a comprehension that exceeds our own power to evoke or even to understand why both God and the dead are so silent. Then it dawns on us that they are near us precisely in our feast of the holy souls. God's silence is the boundless sphere where alone our love can produce its act of faith in his love. If in our earthly life his love had become so manifest to us that we would know beyond a shadow of a doubt what we really are, namely God's own beloved, then how could we prove to him the daring courage and fidelity of our love? How could such a fidelity exist at all? How could our love, in the ecstasy of faith, reach out beyond this world into his world and into his heart? He has veiled his love in the stillness of his silence so that our love might reveal itself in faith. He has apparently forsaken us so that we can find him.

For if his presence in our midst were obvious, in our search for him we would find only ourselves. We must, however, go out from ourselves, if we are to find him where he is really himself. Because his love is infinite, it can dwell openly and radiantly only in his own infinity; and because he wants to show us his infinite love, he has hidden it from us in our finiteness, whence he calls out to us. Our faith in him is nothing but the dark road in the night between the deserted house of our life with its puny, dimly lit rooms, and the blinding light of his eternal life. His silence in this world is nothing but the earthly appearance of the eternal word of his love.

Our dead imitate this silence. Thus, through silence, they speak to us clearly. They are nearer to us than through all the audible words of love and closeness. Because they have entered into God's life, they remain hidden from us. Their words of love do not reach our ears because they have blended into one with the joyous word of his boundless love. They live with the boundlessness of God's life and with his love, and that is why their love and their life no longer enter the narrow room of our present life. We live a dying life. That is why we experience nothing of the eternal life of the holy dead, the life that knows no death. But just in this very way they also live for us and with us. For their silence is their loudest cry, because it is the echo of God's silence. It is in unison with God's word that it speaks to us.

Over against the loud cries of our drives, and over against the anxious, hasty protestations with which we mortals assure ourselves of our mutual love, God's word enwraps us and all our noisy words in his silence. This is the way his word invites us into his life. This is the way he commands us to relinquish all things in the daring act of loving faith, in order to find our eternal homeland in his life.

And it is precisely in this way that the silence of our dead also calls out to us. They live in his life, and that is why they speak his words to us. They speak the word of the God of the true life, the word that is far removed from our dying. The dead are silent because they live, just as our noisy chatter is supposed to make us forget that we are dying. Their silence is the word of their love for us, the real message that they have for us. By this word they are really near to us, provided only that we listen to this soundless word and understand it, and do not drown it out through the noise of everyday life.

It is in this way that they are close to us whose feast we celebrate today in the silent composure of the heart. They are near us together with the silent God, the God of the silent dead, the living God of the living. He calls out to us through his silence, and they, by their silence, summon us into God's life.

Let us therefore be mindful of our dead, our living. Our love for them, our loyalty to them is the proof of our faith in him, the God of everlasting life. Let us not ignore the silence of the dead, the silence that is the most ardent word of their love. This, their most ardent word, accompanies us today and every day, for they have gone away from us in order that their love, having gone into God, may be all the closer to us.

Be mindful of the dead, O heart. They live. Your own life,

the life still hidden even to you, they live unveiled in eternal light. Our living who are with the God of life cannot forget us dead. God has granted our living everything, for he has given them himself. But he goes further and also grants them this favor: that their silence will become the most eloquent word of their love for us, the word that will accompany our love home to them, into their life and their light.

If we really celebrate All Saints and All Souls as the feast of faith, of love, of quiet remembering; if our life is and is always becoming more and more a life of the dead who have gone before us in the sign of faith into the dark night of death, where no man can work; then through God's grace our life becomes, more and more, a life of faith in his light during the night of this earthly life. Then we who are dying live with the living who have gone before us into the bright, shining day of life, where no one has to work, because God himself is this day, the fullness of all reality, the God of the living.

Today or tomorrow, when we stand by the graves, or when our heart must seek distant graves, where perhaps not even a cross stands over them any longer; when we pray, "Lord, grant them eternal rest, and may perpetual light shine upon them"; when we quietly look up towards the eternal homeland of all the saints and—from afar and yet so near—greet God's light and his love, our eternal homeland; then all our memories and all our prayers are only the echo of the words of love that the holy living, in the silence of their eternity, softly and gently speak into our heart. Hidden in the peace of the eternal God, filled with his own bliss, redeemed for eternity, permeated with love for us that can never cease, they, on their feast, utter the prayer of their love for us: "Lord, grant eternal rest to them whom we love—as never before—in your love. Grant it to them who still walk the hard road of pilgrimage, which is nonetheless the road that leads to us and to your eternal light. We, although silent, are now closer to them than ever before, closer than when we were sojourning and struggling along with them on earth. Grant to them, too, Lord, eternal rest, and may your perpetual light shine on them as on us. May it shine upon them now as the light of faith, and then in eternity, as the light of blessed life."

Be mindful of the dead, O heart. Call them into your heart today, listen to their silence, learn from them the one thing necessary: celebrate the feast of your saints. For then the God of all the living will be mindful of us who are dead, and he will one day be our life, too. And there will be one, single, eternal feast of all the saints.